T0128158

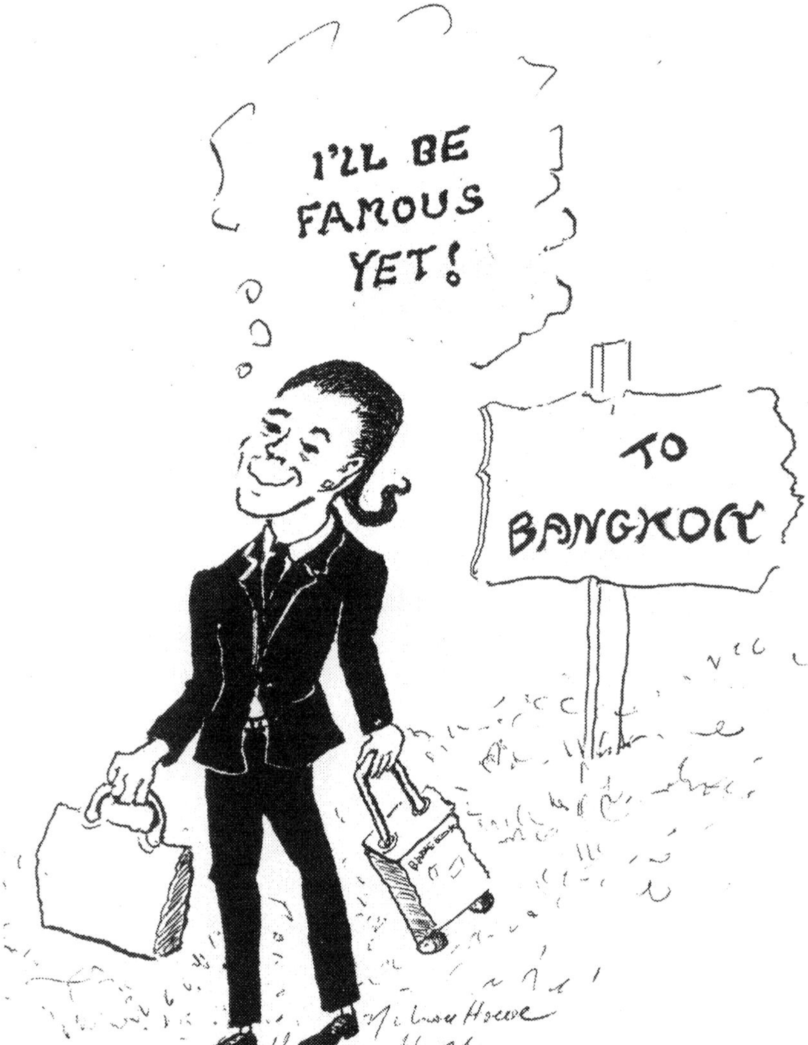

I'LL BE FAMOUS YET!
TO BANGKOK

# MY ADVENTURES IN BANGKOK

## THE STORY OF JOHN, JOHN, JOHN
### NELSON S. HOWE

iUniverse®

MY ADVENTURES IN BANGKOK
THE STORY OF JOHN, JOHN, JOHN

iUniverse books may be ordered through booksellers or by contacting:

iUniverse
1663 Liberty Drive
Bloomington, IN 47403
www.iuniverse.com
1-800-Authors (1-800-288-4677)

ISBN: 978-1-5320-1330-0 (sc)
ISBN: 978-1-5320-1331-7 (e)

Library of Congress Control Number: 2016921206

Print information available on the last page.

iUniverse rev. date: 01/10/2017

This book is dedicated to Benz Thanachart Siripatrachai
my 'adventure' guru and script genius, who kept me out of
mischief, created this opportunity that has changed my life,
and for making my wonderful Bangkok adventure possible.

**With All My Thanks, Gratitude, and Love**
to **Lillian Howe**, my loving wife, for her patience, skilled advice
and proof reading, kind support, and continuing encouragement.

**My Gratitude and Thanks for**
**Noi Pilanda**, for wonderful documentation, continual
caring attention, and for treating me as a king.

**Vichai Matakul**, for his devoted answering of my endless questions,
ensuring my happiness, and total safety while in Bangkok.

**My Thanks and Appreciation:**

Ms **Nok**, the most gracious and generous hostess in Bangkok.

**Toast**, who adopted us, guided us, and showed us the city, even accompanied us to the airport on our last days in Bangkok.

**Lama Shardrol Wangmo**, for her generous editing, and technical help.

**Ruth Grill**, for early shaping and editing my writing.

**Pamela Mc Callister**, for help with final editing.

**Tomsir B. Sylla**, for his brilliant last-minute technological help.

**Salmon House Publishing**, for totally underwriting my stay and making my adventures possible; and wonderful staff who made this unforgettable adventure a total joy.

To the *iUniverse* staff, my gratitude for making this book possible, and the process a pleasure.

# *PREFACE*

In BKK 1st Time, there is a scripted video on You Tube in which I play a philosophy Professor who has mastered the Thai language. It creates my character, and my mastery of the Thai language.

For example, in Thailand, to tease each other, young children repeat the last name of their victim's father in a teasing pattern of three. On screen, I answer Benz, my interviewer, by giving "John" as my father's last name. Benz, asks, would you be upset if I tease you with "John, John, John"?

I say, "No, of course not." He then proceeds to repeat this in a taunting voice until I visibly show increasing anger. Finally, I say a curse word common in Thailand. You can see my response on the book cover.

# 1

## *A Freebie*

"NELSON! YOU'RE INVITED TO BANGKOK, all expenses paid. Lillian's included."

That's from my Thai friend, Benz. He's back in Bangkok now. He made that invitation come true. His full Thai name is Thanachart Siripatrachai. I just call him by his nickname Benz. It's a lot easier.

Some months before the invitation, he made my video *BKK 1ˢᵗ Time* on *You Tube*. It went **viral – over four million** views!

Some of you have seen it already. In it, I play a philosophy professor who's been teaching in Bangkok long enough to curse in Thai. I'm convincing! We create that video right here in New York City.

To my surprise, it leads to national fame in Thailand.

**But I'll tell you a secret. I almost don't make it!**

In Thailand, Benz begins to set up my visit to Bangkok.

Meanwhile, I'm in serious trouble! I need two overnight emergency room treatments in one week to save my feet. The infections are that stubborn . . . <u>very</u> serious.

By the time Benz calls me from Bangkok to have Lillian and I make the trip, I had been in treatment for nearly two months. I had to think about it seriously.

**So why did he invite me to come to Bangkok in the first place?**

It's because my good friend Benz had come into my life.

He videoed a series of my professional dance performances in New York City.

**And that was just the start.**

1

Years earlier, I created, produced, and acted in my martial arts show, *Way of Action,* touring ten years from Texas to Vermont. It even played in New York City and was featured on national television in the David Susskind Show.

Knowing that, Benz had me star in his short film, **The Words I Love.**

To my surprise and pleasure, it was accepted in twelve National Film festivals that played from Alaska to New York. It won three Festival Awards!

He had me learn a Thai dance. He put that on *You Tube* where it gained over seven hundred thousand viewers. (He knew I had toured internationally for three years in a modern dance company, as well as professionally dancing solo for a decade.)

**And <u>then</u> it happened!**

With all that help from Benz, *Salmon House Publishing* in Bangkok wanted me to come make a series of videos for them. These were also for publication on *You Tube.* And by the way, those videos are still playing.

Meanwhile, he wrote about me in one chapter of each of his books, *New York First Time*, and *Real Alaska*. After I got to Bangkok, both became best sellers at the *National Book Fair* in Bangkok.

However, it was **BKK 1ˢᵗ Time** on *You Tube* that forged my national fame in Thailand.

**But I almost didn't make the visit to Bangkok. It was <u>SO</u> close!**

I'd been in treatment for several months. I was still struggling to heal the open wounds on both my ankles.

Just after Benz called, I make my usual weekly visit to my Doctor's office in the *Wound Center* in Manhattan. The Doctor finished wrapping gauze and compression bandages from my toes to my knees on both feet. When I'm about to exit the examination table, I mention, "I'm leaving in about two days for Bangkok. I plan to spend at least a month, or more."

He frowns. "Out of the country for a month, or possibly more?"

I nod agreement.

"I recommend you keep these bandages in place during your whole trip. The medications are essential to prevent your infections from going to the bone."

"What if that happens?"

He stares at me a moment. "For your sake, I hope that doesn't happen. But in case it does, you'll have to be hospitalized for at least a month, or more, on intravenous antibiotics."

He pauses, shakes his head, and continues, "Or worse yet, if that hospital treatment fails, you will have surgical removal of your feet to save your legs . . . **or you could even lose your life!**"

Finally, I catch my breath. "Thank you Doctor. Believe me, I'll make sure I keep my bandages in place for my whole trip!"

# 2

## *DECISION, DECISION, DECISION!*

IT'S A QUANDARY – GO to Bangkok, or stay home?

My Doctor who warned me, as well as Lillian and my sister, are the chorus with the same song. "Don't risk your life!"

I already know about that. "It's still **my decision!"**

Then, Lillian, and my sister add another opinion. They point to the military coup in May this same year.

"How safe is it to be there about four months after the military takes over? There could be continued fighting."

I tell her, "Coups are routine in Thai history. All's quiet there now. A successful routine coup will not stop me from going – and neither will the sores on my ankles."

Then, my sister reads several books about Thailand. The phone rings again.

I almost don't pick it up.

"So *now* what is it?"

"There's a criminal element in Thailand! You could be kidnapped for money, or sold into slavery, or even killed! It's too dangerous for you to go!"

"It's dangerous here too". "I've lived in New York City since 1961. I've faced knife threats, gangs and gun fights outside in the street, and organized crime in several neighborhoods already.

I'm still here. I was lucky. Besides, Benz isn't afraid to live in Bangkok. He isn't even a trained martial artist."

The next evening, at dinner with Lillian, I spell it out.

"I'm certain now. If I don't accept the invitation to Bangkok, I'll regret it for the rest of my life. I'd much rather die on an adventure than moldering in my room for the rest of my life. Why not enjoy a country where millions already know me, and nearly ten thousand people are friending me on Face Book?"

So, as we finish our chocolate cake at dinner that evening, I ask Lillian, "Are you going with me, or not?"

Without hesitation, she answers, "I won't let you leave without me!"

# 3

## *THE DECISION*

THAT EVENING AFTER DINNER AND the TV news, she tells me, "I want to see Bangkok for a second time in my life. The first time was part of a five-year adventure in my early twenties."

As we sat together on the couch, she shared stories of her travels across Europe, Australia, the mid-east, India, Thailand, and beyond. Much of her journey was on foot, alone as a young, single woman. She had taken amazing risks.

She tells me, "This time, we will both leave on our adventure together. It's a great opportunity. We can't miss it. We'll be going half way around the world together. And this is our first time in *both* our lives!"

And we're both delighted.

However, in the last few days before we leave, she begins to look rather preoccupied.

Just before leaving, she tells me. "Nelson, you know I want to go with you, but as I think about it, I can't take more than a week away from here. I have to continue working on my designs for the jewelry shows. The deadlines are very close."

"I know it's disappointing, but I hope you understand."

"I understand, but I'm surprised too."

Given her five years of traveling half way across the world when she was in her early twenties, I expected her to spend at least two full weeks in Bangkok. But this is a very different time in her life. She's older, and she's totally devoted to her jewelry designing and shows. I know it's important. She's making the most of remaining time in her life.

And so am I.

I tell her, "I'm also disappointed. I'm sorry we can't spend more time on this vacation together, As I think about it, however. It's wonderful you're choosing to come half way around the world for a short week with me.

I think about it and point out, "It's a gift . . . and a long way to go. At least you'll be with me to start. I'm happy you'll be with me for the beginning."

I thought everything was settled but in the last days before the flight, one more possible difficulty appears.

Several health professionals caution me.

"Since there's a minimum of at least a twenty-two-hour flight each way, you'll need to move around every two hours to prevent blood clots. Because of your advanced age, you're especially susceptible with your infected wounds and possible blood clots. People sometimes die from it. Even if you live, it can ruin your life."

I'll easily solve that risk, once I'm on the plane. Just like home, I'll get up about every two hours, day and night. I'll make a point of sitting in the aisle seat to make it even easier.

# 4

## *OUR 30 HOUR BEGINNING*

AND, FLY WE DO – twenty-two hours in the air plus a six-hour layover in Shanghai.

We arrive after **twenty-eight hours**. It's the evening of September 28th, 2014. After our landing, Lillian borrows a wheelchair. We go to the luggage carousel where I manage to grab our two, worn, antique suitcases. She leaves her borrowed wheelchair behind and returns to using her cuff crutch to limp toward the exit. I'm managing to limp along with her in spite of my compression bandages on both legs.

As we hobble out to see if our hosts are there waiting for us, it feels as if we've been dragged through a war.

We must look bedraggled, but HOORAY! In the vast reaches of the airport, the enthusiastic staff from Salmon Publishing recognizes us. We're delighted!

They're excited. We've made it! It feels like we're their long-lost Auntie and Uncle from outer space, and they cluster around us for a joyous welcome, and their self-introductions.

Neither of us are able to remember any of their names after so many hours of travel. We consider ourselves lucky to remember our own names. We do recall seeing Benz. Later we learn, Noi, the Producer, Vichai who will be my guide, and Toast who took us out shopping and often accompanied us on other outings, were also there.

To our relief, the greeting is simple, joyous, and short. Then, we're whisked into a waiting van.

"This will be a bit of a drive," they tell us, and quickly, we're out of the airport onto a four-lane expressway.

Lillian and I are both very tired . . . but far too excited to be dozing off.

As we near the city, traffic becomes dense and slows us to a near crawl. What we assume is a defective stoplight about halfway through the drive, adds to a seemingly endless trip.

Later, Vichai explains, "This is usual. It could have been a lot worse. For example, "I was trying to get in to work one morning when I got stuck at that light. It was a three-hour traffic jam."

I think maybe he's trying to convince us we got lucky, and I'll take his word on that! We did!"

# 5

## *HITTING THE HAY*

FINALLY, OUR VAN COMES TO a stop in the hotel parking lot. Gratefully, the staff hauls our luggage along with us up to our hotel room. We're very pleased to see the spacious room has a large double bed, complete bathroom, plenty of storage, a desk, and a table for eating. Nearby, there's a full- size refrigerator, a big television set, and at that hour in our trip, an especially inviting leather covered black couch.

When we express surprise at the refrigerator and dishes, they tell us, "it's a residential hotel." Clearly, it's now our home away from home. No stove, but the staff came prepared. They put food in the refrigerator for that night, and the next day. They also include a canister of potato chips, and a canister of peanuts with a coconut coating. Those peanuts became a favorite of mine for the rest of the trip – super good!

There's also an assortment of other snack foods on the cabinet top. Nothing was overlooked.

Having arranged for our comfort, our welcoming committee says their "good night" and assures us, "we'll come for you tomorrow at two in the afternoon."

Lillian and I unpack our necessities, use our toothbrushes, and she showers after the trip. I'm bandaged from toes to knees on both legs. I was told not to get those bandages wet, so I do a 'stand up' washcloth cleanup. That washcloth method was required for the entire time of the trip.

As we prepare for bed, it feels comfortably cool in the room.

"Lillian, look up there – must be air conditioning!"

Surprised, she exclaims. "It's coming in up along the ceiling!"

I go look out on the balcony and sure enough, the machine itself is sitting there and the cooled air is brought in along the ceiling with a conduit.

I come off the balcony and tell Lillian, "That's really smart – not like the positioning of air conditioners in most US homes and hotels. The cold air blows directly on us there."

Grateful, and half asleep by that time, we fall into bed. It turns out to be a very comfortable night indeed, and we quickly slip into a much-needed sleep.

# 6

## *AMAZING*

THE BED'S HEAVEN, ESPECIALLY AFTER our efforts in the plane seats. It's the sleep of the dead. Sunshine streams in from the balcony – both of us wake up, totally alert. We check our clock and it's just after six in the morning. We dress, and are ready to go out to hunt for breakfast. As we are about to leave, there's a timid knock on our door.

"Who the hell dares to knock at this hour," I mumble.

On the way to the door, I'm grumbling, "Barely morning yet! They must have insomnia. "They told us they're coming for us at two pm. I want my breakfast at least."

At that point, I'm tempted to make a loud snoring sound to pretend we're still sleeping but we give each other 'the look' to be sure we're both properly dressed.

Lillian yawns, and begins making the bed as I open the door.

It's a delivery man. He hands me a bag, bows and leaves even before I can manage a "thank you."

"Lillian, it's our breakfast. How could they know we're up . . . <u>and</u> HUNGRY?"

Lillian is placing the silverware and dishes and tells me, "I don't know about you, but I'm up for this every morning. I don't care how they know."

I start opening the package. "Hey, even the coffee's in here, already made! It's incredible room service!"

Lillian smiles as she finishes setting the table. "It's our first breakfast in Bangkok. We haven't even ordered in!"

"Awesome," I exclaim, adjusting my napkin, as I sit down to eat. "How could they have known we got up so early? They certainly must have known when we arrived. The room must be bugged.

"I don't care, as long as it gets here on time – and a good breakfast too," She tells me.

"I agree," I say, as I finish my second waffle with syrup. "With service like this, they must fill the place all the time."

"Lillian gets up and starts clearing the dishes. "It's really good. I already wish I don't have to leave so soon."

"I'm sorry too," and I get up and come over to her for a hug and a kiss. "I'm sorry it's such a short vacation for us. I'll miss you."

During the rest of Lillian's visit, and all of my stay, the food is a continuing gift with a wide variety, excellent nutrition. It's always provided for our convenience and pleasure. In fact, the food preparers here in Bangkok are amazing. They provide the meal as soon as we begin to feel hungry.

After we finish unpacking, we go out on the balcony for our first look over the city.

Oooh! It's hot out here, I exclaim."

"And not at all cool out here like our room," Lillian responds as she heads back in and turns on the television. As I come back in, she informs me, "The daily temperature now in late October, is averaging the mid-eighties! And it's that now already this morning.

Having finished our breakfast, done the dishes, and tidied up the room, we go out into the hall to take the elevator down. We almost miss it. That's because there are three elevator doors available. There's no light above the doors to indicate which elevator is activated, so, without warning, the far one happens to come open first. We discover they close fast, and we aren't so fast on our feet.

Fortunately, I'm still somewhat agile in spite of my bandages. I block the door with my arm. The two stubborn doors try desperately to perform an amputation on it. They tire quickly and I manage to get my foot in the way as they attempt this maneuver again. They aren't as devious as they appeared or they would have held on to my foot.

I discover later, they could be choosy, and one of them held my leg until Lillian was finally able to convince it to let me go.

# 7

## YOU'D NEVER GUESS

WE DECIDE TO EXPLORE BANGKOK before our two o'clock appointment with the staff.

We exit the elevator. We limp through the rather large lobby past the four desk clerks who abruptly stand up at attention and bow to us with their hands together, prayer style, in front of their faces.

I turn to Lillian. "Maybe they do this for everybody?

"I don't know. Must be."

I take a quick look around. "Nobody else."

"So it must be us," Lillian replies.

We smile politely and say "hello." They return the "hello" and remain standing stiffly at attention.

Assuming formalities are finished, we continue blithely toward a glass door at the far end of the room. It appears to lead to the street.

As we walk toward it, we notice the lobby's well furnished, with a large leather covered sofa, several soft overstuffed chairs, a newspaper and magazine center, and four more overstuffed chairs.

"Inviting," I comment, "in case I want to catch up on the news,"

"It can probably wait until some other time," Lillian replies as we approach the door.

It springs open, as I reach out to open it. I pull my extended arm back. Only then, I notice a well-groomed man in a tan uniform on the other side of the glass door. He bows slightly with prayer-like hands in front of his face, much like the desk clerks do.

As we pass through the doorway, our uniformed door-opener seems to have a slight smile.

Of course, we both say, "thank you." and are nearly drowned out by a thunderous roar from the street.

# 8

## *ZOWIE!*

THE NARROW STREET IN FRONT of us is a two-lane torrent of traffic. It's rushing frantically in both directions – fender to fender – packed in the bottom of the narrow canyon of buildings – desperately racing to find an emergency exit.

I look around. No one's paying any attention to the uproar, or to us either, so I try to make sense of it all. In front of us is this virtual army of cars, people, and motorcycles roaring past in both directions. I turn to Lillian and shout above the noise, **"unbelievable!"**

Lillian stares speechless for a moment and shouts above the roar, **"Thousands of them! But look, people are walking there too – no sidewalk!"**

Then shouts, **"Something's missing – no police cars – no fire engines – no ambulances!**

**"Yah, and no sirens, and no horns blaring."**

I can't believe this torrent of vehicles manages to race in both directions at the same time without collisions.

I holler, **"That's astounding! There's not even a white line down the middle!"**

I hear Lillian shouting, **"It's an incredible show, like in a Carnival!"**

I can't resist. I take out my *iPhone* and snap a few frames of traffic.

We both stand mesmerized by the performance and finally, Lillian comes out of her trance, **"Look, Nelson, there's even a 7-Eleven store down the road!"**

**"A 7-Eleven?"** I wake up again. **"You're joking! 7-Elevens are in small town America. How could one of those get all the way here? You must be kidding."**

**"What?! McDonald's are all over the world, why wouldn't Bangkok have a 7-Eleven?**

I look carefully. And sure enough, she's right . . . again.

**"So you want to go there,"** I ask.

**"Yes,"** she shouts.

**"That store is on the other side of the canyon! I don't think it's safe to try to cross this street – too much raging traffic."**

**"I know, but there must be a way to cross over."**

**". . . no crossing at the corners. No stop signs! No light either! I'm too young to die,"** I shout back.

Lillian takes my hand. **"Ok, let's join the circus! Will we be clowns, or lions?"**

**"Whatever we are,"** I shout back, **"our first act is jay walkers."**

We both laugh.

"Ok," I holler back, "**Let's go! It should be spectacular with your crutch.**"

"**Thanks! Let's look for an opening.**"

She lets go of my hand. We continue walking along on our precarious edge of disaster with the traffic while we continue to look for an opening. I'm getting nervous as I watch her hobble with barely inches between the racing vehicles and her arm. She continues nonchalantly ahead of me.

Traffic continues to prove how close cars and motorcycles can come without grazing her elbow, or worse – mine too, for that matter.

While I'm trying to think what to do about that, Lillian suddenly shouts, "**We need to cross now! Right after that car!**"

I shout over the roar of traffic. "**Not right here I hope.**" But then I see the opening on our side.

We both step into the street. Traffic coming in the other direction is slowing.

"**Amazing, they're making room for us! They must see your crutch!**"

I stay next to her for my self-protection as we hobble across.

As we reach the other side, I holler, "**We probably set the all-time record for interrupting traffic on that street.**"

Then I hear Lillian's voice, "**It must also be a record for vehicles with caring humans in them.**"

I take Lillian's hand for a moment as I ask, "**Shall we try to book the act now, or do we need more practice?**"

"**Let's give it another try going back. We may need to perfect it.**"

# 9

## MAYBE NEW SPEAK

WITH RELIEF, WE REACH THE 7-Eleven unscathed, and there's a small cement sidewalk in front of it too, so I stop, take out my *iPhone* and try to get more shots of the traffic. At that moment, I see a motorcycle with a woman sidesaddle on the back and I shout, **"Look! She's a star – it's a sidesaddle show!"**

I fumble with the *iPhone* and push the wrong button. The woman is carrying her infant son in one arm and holding on to the seat with the other hand as they swerve in and out of the traffic. No photo.

**"Oh shit!"** I shout, "wait 'til I tell my sister about this."

Lillian shakes her head, **"Don't bother, nobody'll believe you anyway."**

As we enter the 7-Eleven, it looks like we're back in small town America, with an exception we expected. There are almost no labels in English. However, we find we can recognize package contents by their pictures. It's the same method as it is with magazines.

"Since we're staying in the hotel a block away," Lillian points out, "we'll come back when we have a list of things we'll need by then."

With that, we exit back into the madness of street traffic. I shout, **"It's far more exciting than New York City, no lights, and no sidewalks . . . and apparently, no regulations."**

Lillian shouts back, **"Yeah, and we take more risk than a tight rope walker too."**

I agree, but I decide to stay focused on zooming car mirrors and racing motorcycle handle bars right at my elbow.

We make it safely back to the hotel.

As we arrive, the desk staff does its 'stand stiffly' routine, unaware we deserve the national award for extreme naiveté and amazing good luck.

As we will learn later, our friends, hosts, and entire staff will hold themselves responsible if we get hurt. It's hard to believe everyone connected with our visit here has that kind of caring.

# 10

## *WHAT NEXT?*

WE'RE STANDING JUST INSIDE THE lobby. After our discovery of the 7-Eleven, Lillian checks her watch and turns to me.

"We aren't scheduled for a pick up by the studio staff until two o'clock today," Lillian happily reminds me, "and we have four hours yet before they come to see us."

"We're **free**! Let's go look around some more!"

She nods, "better check in at the desk. Maybe there's a place to shop."

The desk clerks stand again, bowing politely.

I make my self-created bow, while Lillian asks, "Any way to get to a good Department Store besides walking?"

The clerk politely responds with a "Yes," in English and looks at her watch. Looking rather uneasy, she tells us, "There's a van leaving the hotel for the *Rama Shopping Center* in five minutes." She emphasizes her next sentence. "The van returns every hour, on the hour also. It's free and it stops at the door there," as she points across the room.

I look where she's pointing. I hadn't been aware of that door before.

I turn back and almost in unison, Lillian and I say, "Oh, perfect!"

With that, the desk staff all sit down again. We smile, wave, and go out to stand on the little cement 'landing pad' and congratulate ourselves. We still have time before the studio staff is due at 2:00 pm, and ten minutes later, we're in the hotel van watching the streets go by.

In less than a half hour, our van delivers us to the *Rama Shopping Mall*. I'm not sure whether to tip the van driver when he comes around our side to open our door for us.

Lillian explains to me, "since we're hotel guests and the driver works for the hotel, he gets paid for driving each way every hour, anyway. It's not like a taxi driver in America who makes a special trip for each person and depends on tips as an important part of his pay for the day."

# 11

## *LEARNING TO STAR*

AS WE DESCEND FROM THE van, we arrive at a street lined with large stores. The traffic here is heavy and has many more motorcycles than is common back home unless there's a convention for them or it's a large motorcycle gang. As we walk across to check out the stores, we discover we've arrived where the two city subway systems intersect. The huge Department Stores are just across the street.

"Subways! Like New York maybe," I comment, as we stand looking.

Lillian gives me a quick look. "The hotel staff didn't say anything about it as an option for travel. No telling where they go," she comments. "Besides, we have the van."

"You're right. Let's get across traffic and look inside the store."

"It sure is impressive," Lillian replies. "It even has a familiar feeling."

After exploring several stores, we realize it's a mall, and we end up in *Robinson's Department Store*. As we are shopping, a young woman shyly asks, "Are you John, John, John? Nelson?" I respond with my "yes," and a smile.

"Can I have a 'selfie' with you?"

I'm surprised that she remembered the line from my video. The 'selfie' is new for me. Lillian steps aside. My admirer snuggles up beside me so I put my arm around her waist. She hugs even closer and gets both our faces in the shot. Happily thanking me in English, she disappears into the array of clothing displays.

It's not like America . . . and I'm all for that, especially since I assume this is a rare occasion. It feels really good to be hugged, and very good that she remembers the line from the video. But most of all, I feel pleased to be recognized by a total stranger who picks me out of a crowd.

We continue the shopping. I also am identified and I happily comply with the occasional 'selfie' requests.

Between our shopping and the 'selfies,' we manage to stock up on clothes we might need for our stay in the city. And by now, almost three hours have passed. Loaded with our finds in the clothing department and my encounters for 'selfies', we head back to catch the van to the hotel. It's close, but we do a 'hobble run' as best we can, and get to it just in time.

On our arrival, the desk clerks immediately stand stiffly and bow at attention again. This time, they seem genuinely relieved to see us return.

I eventually learn these bows with hands in prayer position are called 'wei's'. These are given at slightly different levels, depending on what degree of respect is appropriate for the person being 'wei'd' to.

I've vowed to do my best to imitate their signs of greeting with my version of a 'wei'. I like to believe my version of it is the same for everyone. I think it's democratic, and they seem very happy . . . or . . . amused may be the better interpretation. I plan to return my imitation of a 'wei' to anyone who does it, anytime it's offered, from now on.

It doesn't seem to require absolute mastery if I remember to smile with it each time. Being able to pay respects in return makes me feel as though I'm integrated into their social norms – even though I know I stand out like a sore thumb.

The obvious clue is my 'costume'. I'm the only man in the whole city who's formally dressed in business attire. It does have one small advantage. It's very comfortable in our air-conditioned hotel room. However, it's uncomfortably hot out on the street at eighty-five degrees. I'm immediately seen as an 'old farang geezer', as the Thai press has it.

I tell myself, I'm a star with over four million viewers, so wherever I go, I need to be wearing my 'costume'. I wore that one for the video Benz created. He insisted I bring it when I came to Bangkok.

After all, an opportunity to be a star doesn't come along just every day – not for me, anyway.

# 12

## *ABANDONED?*

WHEN LILLIAN AND I GET back to our room, we barely have time to unpack our suitcases before the hotel delivery person knocks on our door with our lunch. As is becoming usual, his timing is uncanny. He makes a formal bow as he hands me the package. This time, I'm prepared to bow. However, as I take the package, he then returns my bow by bowing with prayer position of his hands at face level.

Now, I suddenly have a problem. How do I return a bow with both hands since my left hand is now holding our lunch? I have no idea what to do, so I raise my right hand up beside my nose as I say, "thank you". The deliveryman shows just a hint of suppressed amusement as he politely turns and walks back to the elevators.

As I close the door, I can't think of any way to solve the bowing process when receiving a package. I plan to ask Benz. Courtesy has suddenly gotten complicated. I'm not sure whether to follow Lillian's example and skip the formal respectful bowing, or do it and look like I'm being something of the City Clown. I decide on the latter choice. I figure, maybe I'll be given some extra social points for making the effort, even one handed. So far, most people have smiled. That's encouraging.

After our American style lunch was delivered, enjoyed, and the remains cleaned up, we spend time with small talk. As two o'clock approaches, we're beginning to substitute the small talk with fidgeting.

Two o'clock comes and goes. No one calls for us. We wonder if there's a mistake. Maybe we should call Noi or Benz, but we don't know their phone numbers. Should we call the desk and get the number? Maybe we misunderstood? Or maybe they forgot.

# 13

## COMING 'UPPANCE'

WE'RE ABOUT TO CALL THE desk and the phone rings. It's the desk clerk saying, "Your ride is waiting for you." We press the button for an elevator and go back down the eight floors.

"They didn't forget after all."

Lillian nods with a smile.

A small group with Noi, Benz, Vichai, May, Toast, and several other staff members from the studio are gathered near the side door to the hotel parking area.

I greet them with, "Hello everyone!"

Their first comment after greeting us was, "We thought you'd still be asleep."

We probably both look puzzled. Asleep at this hour, they think? Maybe they think we're on our honeymoon.

They notice our puzzlement and say, "You know . . . jet lag?"

I respond with, "nope, no jet lag."

They look surprised.

"We were up at six this morning." Then to be sure all is clear, I announce confidently, "And, we went shopping."

The group suddenly appears even more concerned. "You've been shopping?"

The one who asked, seems especially upset.

"Sure," I answer proudly, "Robinson's Department Store!"

My comment is followed by a heavy silence. Everyone seems to have been suddenly struck speechless.

Then, as if I've committed some kind of major indiscretion, Benz, approaches me, and staring at me, finally asks, "The two of you went alone?"

I decide I must have said something wrong. But what was it? Whatever it was, I realize the person asking if we went alone was quite upset. I decide to clarify it with more detail.

"Yes, first we went to the 7-Eleven down the street. Then, we took the hotel van to the *Rama Center*. When we got there, we shopped for a while. Lillian and I were together. We weren't alone there."

Now the whole group looks really shocked. Benz takes me aside and says seriously, "Don't ever go out without one of us with you again You need to call us first. Just call one of us and we'll come pick you up!"

I decide to explain why we felt so safe. "We did take the hotel van," assuming that was acting totally in protocol.

Benz looks very serious, shakes his head slightly, and says, "It's not the **same!** Always call **us** before you go out. Lillian and I are upset, but it's later when we wonder, "How do we call them?"

# 14

## MEANS WHAT?

LATER THAT DAY, THEY TAKE us back to the *Rama Shopping Mall* in their car. We're surprised because I had already told them, "We bought a few things there."

When we get to the Rama Mall, they drive up inside, one level after another. I haven't been in every American City, but I never encountered interior parking that went up, maybe ten floors or even more. In most American shopping malls, there are no interior ramps. All the parking is outside the store on ground level. Or, in cities like New York City, or Chicago, there are multi-level parking garages nearby where we pay, or we park on the street at meters and risk expensive parking tickets.

As we go upward above the tenth floor or so, we get glimpses of the city as if we're flying. Even up at that level, the parking area is stuffed with hundreds and hundreds of cars. As I recall, Vichai searched several very long isles. No luck. He continues going up until he finally locates a place to park on what I believe is the fourteenth floor.

We all get out and walk together into the store. While Lillian and I begin a second round of perusing the now familiar merchandise, Benz and the group immediately start wandering around on the same floor. When we ask, they tell us they're just browsing. They happily leave us with the assurance, "We'll come back and let you know if anything interesting turns up."

As Lillian and I begin our own wandering, I wonder if Vichai can remember how to find the car again. I certainly have no idea.

The group returns soon without suggestions. I'm relieved.

Meanwhile, I'm approached by a young lady who recognizes me from the *You Tube Video*. She's excited by her discovery and wants her 'selfie' with me. She hands the camera to Benz and cuddles up to my side. Lillian and the group from the studio move slightly away, as if they're choreographed as the audience. She cuddles up and I put my arm around her waist while she put up her hand with her first two fingers apart in a V shape. I did the same and we both smile for the camera.

She smiles at the results, thanks us, and is lost in the crowd.

I have no idea what the V means unless it comes from *World War Two,* when it meant V for Victory over the Axis powers. Maybe she felt victorious just because her wish came true, to have her selfie with me. Later, Lillian and I agree, "that must be what it means."

Within the week, I discover there are many hand signals, each with a particular Thai meaning. I simply make the same signal my 'snuggle' uses, whatever it is. It seems to work well. My 'fan' is pleased.

# 15

## *IT SURE AIN'T THE USA*

IN AMERICA, ON THE RARE occasion when anyone ever came close enough for a photo with me, they went sideways – hip to hip, with both of us front facing . . . if we touched our hips together at all.

Here in Bangkok, a "Selfie" seems to be much more affectionate, more a 'snuggle' than a similar encounter would be in America. Don't get me wrong. I love it. Please continue this way. I'm all for it.

For several weeks I tried to find out why there was this difference between the two cultures. I was finally told, it's because I'm old, and not a threat anymore.

Okay, that will do. It's a small price for a nice snuggle. I know I'm not a Clark Gable or a Cary Grant. No one has ever swooned on meeting me . . . so far. I never had a real snuggle with a 'selfie' until I got to Bangkok. It's turning out being old in Bangkok is a real pleasure. I'll be sorry when it comes time to leave it behind.

After the 'selfie', we all go to another floor. Benz and Toast start discussing what I will need for communication during my stay. They had discovered my cell phone only works in the hotel on Wi-Fi there.

They decide I need a new phone for my visit so they can call me when they have a message for me. Likewise, I can reach them if I have a question or need transportation. Benz and the group abandon us on the electronics floor to continue their shopping.

It's been a long day. Lillian and I already agree, "we're finished, totally shopped out!" We continue to wander for what seems miles around the vast floor, but there's no place to sit down. So, we continue aimlessly sleepwalking, desperately hoping we find something that might serve as a place to rest our feet. No luck.

Finally, we stagger about looking at television sets. Still no place to sit down. The group doesn't return to keep us entertained. We decide to remain in the area where they abandoned us. We're concerned about becoming lost. Still, no place to sit, except on the floor. By that time, we're so tired, we're not sure either one of us could get up, even if we sat in a chair.

Finally, they arrive after another hour or so. By that time, we're walking zombies. They excitedly announced a decision to buy a *Samsung Android* phone for my use, whatever that is. Lillian and I aren't very savvy about smartphones.

Benz announces, "We used the time to program it with photos of us. That way if one of us doesn't answer, you can reach any of the other five staff members. Just call if you need anything."

I'm impressed. That turns out to be a very useful and considerate temporary loan. Along with their names, and phone numbers, there is a photo portrait of each one with their title, such as *Graphics*, or *Publicity*. Benz pointed out, "That's so you will learn to recognize us by name, as well as position in the company."

If that phone had been in hand when we began the trip to the store, we would have called them several hours ago.

From then on, it proves to be very helpful. I carry that phone with me the rest of the visit . . . and I return it at the airport, the very day I leave.

# 16

## *I Forget Emily Post*

WHEN WE RETURN TO OUR hotel room, we discover an invitation for dinner later that evening from Ms Nok. We're assured there's time to change into proper attire for the occasion and of course, we gladly accept her invitation. She's our hostess.

We're both especially excited about meeting her, as totally wiped out as we both are. However, we had no idea there was to be a very formal occasion that evening. Fortunately, we had brought suitable clothes just for such an occasion.

In my case, my costume is for every occasion. No problem. I have this occasion covered also, so to speak.

We're picked up by car and driven to the restaurant dressed in our best clothes. The large parking area is filled with expensive cars, and crowds of well-dressed couples who politely crowd with us toward the main entrance.

As we arrive in the front entry, we're introduced to Ms Nok. We learn she's head of *Salmon House*, the company that will publish the videos on *You Tube*. We also meet one of her sons at the dinner and discover she has another son and several daughters, all of whom I met in the following weeks.

Ms. Nok speaks perfect English, very gracious, slim, with beautiful posture and a very elegant evening dress. As she talks briefly with us, we find we're not just her guests. We're her guests of honor. As I learn during my six weeks, she's very kind, generous, and from this night on, I'm convinced, she's the perfect hostess.

After meeting her, we're taken to a large private dining room with a giant roundtable. We're led to our appointed seats with our place names on them. We're introduced to seven or eight others, most of whom are the people I would be meeting later during my stay. Our friend Benz, is seated next to me on my right, with Lillian on my left. I'm grateful to be in the middle of this protective sandwich, especially since most of the people at the table are already happily conversing in Thai, even Benz . . . except when he makes a frequent point of talking to Lillian and me.

I feel very awkward. It's been years since I was part of any kind of large very formal gathering. Here, I'm a special guest at a very formal occasion and I really only know the two people who sit on each side of me. Everyone else except Benz and Lillian are strangers.

I vaguely remember Emily Post and read her book cover to cover when I was in High School. I forgot most of it but I recalled it is polite to talk some of the time to the person on my right, but be sure to also give sufficient time to the person on my left.

I'm tongue tied, however. I try to remember if Emily Post had any suggestions about my increasing panic. I can't even think what to say to Benz and Lillian, and I act like we never met.

I'm thinking how awkward I feel. I can hear the others speaking on the other side of the table but I can't understand a single word they're saying. To my relief, the first dishes finally arrive on the table. At least, this way I can enter the sensory world which is wonderfully calming. The dishes contain exceptionally delicious Thai cooking, an extraordinary once-in-a-lifetime feast.

Benz instructs the two of us briefly on Thai etiquette. This includes the Thai method of eating with our fork in our left hand and the large tablespoon held in our right hand. I was born left handed but was forced at birth to switch to my right hand, so that didn't seem so strange. But at this very formal meal it begins to feel a bit awkward now, all of a sudden.

Benz had taught me this method in Thai restaurants in Brooklyn and New York City during the year and a half we had come to know each other. I hadn't become particularly proficient with the method yet, and being a creature of habit, often abandoned the large tablespoon altogether, changing my fork back to my right hand. During most of the dinner I manage to follow Thai custom without switching over.

Rather than trying to incorporate the new way to eat, Lillian very wisely proceeds to use her fork, even though it's elegantly prepared Thai food.

# 17

## *EMILY POST IN BANGKOK*

AS THE MEAL PROGRESSES, I gradually begin to relax. I talk briefly with Benz, and with Lillian. Each of the dishes is truly delicious, and as soon as one goes around the table, another takes its place. I try to sample each one. It's a gourmet feast. I counted well over twenty separate dishes before I finally gave up during our several hours at the table. It's impossible to sample every single one. I never heard of a dinner with that many courses, except the Roman orgies, and I'm getting stuffed. I'm not seventeen anymore. Besides, I can't eat as fast as I did when I started.

However, late in the dinner, I begin to struggle with my attempt to eat in the Thai tradition, the spoon in my right hand, and the fork in my left. Soon, I'm unlearning the method and begin to eat with the wrong utensil. Thinking it will probably go unnoticed, I finally take a piece of fish in my fingers from my main plate, and quickly place it on my side plate.

Shocked silence – all conversation stops mid-sentence. Everyone sees me do it! I freeze. It feels like an hour is passing while I sit in speechless terror. I well know it would be impolite, even shocking in such a dinner in America too. Finally, Benz announces, "It's not polite to touch the food with your fingers here in Thailand."

I can't decide whether I should instantly jump to my feet and leave the table, or tough it out as the rude American. I figure, if I left the table, I'd probably have to pay for my own airfare and fly home alone. It occurs to me, as a rude American that might happen anyway, but I hope it can be seen as funny and lead to general hilarity.

No luck. I sit there trying to decide whether to apologize and call more attention to it, or just endure the situation in silence. Everyone, including Lillian, is looking down and no one smiles. I feel like we're all sitting in silence for another hour.

I realized the shock wore off in only a few moments during which everyone made note of what I did . . . and what that means about me. They recover from it and go on talking as if the scene on the film had just been edited, as though nothing appears to have happened. With a dinner as good as that one, no one would desire to sit there and sulk about my bad behavior while the food gets cold.

Once I realized I wasn't going home on the next plane just because I had misbehaved, I didn't stop eating. So much for *Emily Post*. She was years before, and I've practiced my disregard of what I read for fifty years. That finally came back to bite me.

My *faux pas* wasn't mentioned again while I was in Bangkok. A picture of me eating with my fingers on a later occasion, appeared on my *Face Book*.

# 18

## HOW DID SHE KNOW?

AFTER OUR GOODBYES TO MS Nok and her guests, we're driven back to our hotel. Lillian and I are now totally stuffed, and sleepwalking. The phone rings before we can undress. It's Noi and several others from the studio. They want to come up to see us for a few minutes. We agree, since everything has become a dream anyway. When they arrive, they give Lillian six beautiful fashion hats with a card from Ms Nok.

Lillian tries each hat on. Everyone excitedly agrees, she looks very elegant in each one. To our amazement, they all fit Lillian perfectly. The impromptu fashion show is a mini party – a perfect ending to a royal welcome. It's dark, and becoming late in the evening.

We ask Noi to please extend our thanks and gratitude to Ms Nok for the lovely hats, and the wonderful dinner. The group hurries out to the elevator.

Alone again in our room, Lillian and I are increasingly aware of our hostess' remarkable generosity and ability to know not only her hat sizes, when to have our breakfasts sent up to our room, but also, her ability to meet needs we didn't even know we had.

For example, why all the hats?

# 19

## *DESPERATION*

WE LEARN THE SIGNIFICANCE OF the gift of hats when we came downstairs in the morning for breakfast. It's a bright, sunny day, as are the next four. In the next few days Lillian finds even more reasons to value the gifts. Somehow, Lillian manages to squeeze all her treasured hats into her small suitcase for their trip to Brooklyn – every one of them.

We pop out of bed, fully awake by six o'clock again this morning, her second day. It's light out. And again, we eat a large American style breakfast delivered to the room, remarkably, just as we are dressed. This time, I bow and 'wei" as I greet the delivery man, take the package of food, and thank him in English. Without further ceremony, he leaves. He doesn't say anything. I assume he hasn't learned English.

Later that morning, Toast and Noi take us shopping for local wares that Lillian might like to take back to Brooklyn. When we finish, we all go to a *Starbucks* coffee shop. The four of us have a chance to get further acquainted. As Toast returns with our orders, a casually dressed man seems to be staring at us from a nearby table. We joke, "no privacy, just like back home."

Lillian and I enjoy the chance to learn more about the schedule of our sightseeing with the guide for the following days. We enjoy talking with Noi and Toast, but Noi soon leaves for the studio and Toast goes out to arrange for the van for us.

As they leave, they indicate that there will be a van across the street at eleven to bring Lillian back to the hotel. It will drop me off at the studio.

Lillian and I discuss what we need to be doing and as we stand up to leave, 'Mr. Staring,' comes over to us and politely asks, "are you 'John' – you know – on *You Tube*?" I nod yes. I notice, here's another one speaking good English. He wants his "selfie" with me to say the Thai curse word, "ku wai!" (You can see my facial expression when I say it on *You Tube*.) Toast was the cameraman for him.

As we move toward the door, two women cross the room now. They decide they guessed right, so each of them has their selfie with me.

It is nearly time to go to the van. Desperate to leave by now, we hurry to the door, just as a young woman hurries in. Another selfie!

We rush out and down the stairs. Thinking we've finally escaped, an older woman catches us.

It's becoming a bad dream.

Risking our lives to cross the street, we barely make it to the van where Toast and the driver are waiting for us.

# 20

# *An Emergency*

AFTER OUR BREAKFAST THE NEXT morning, Linda, our guide arrives at nine to bring us out to her car. She tells us "It's our grand tour of Bangkok, and we'll go on a boat tour this morning."

Lillian will now have a reason to be grateful for the hats.

We spend a relaxing morning on a riverboat built for four.

It's designed, Thai style, shaped at each end like a Tibetan slipper with sharp turned up toes and horizontal stripes in bright colors. As we travel past industrial centers, large estates, and monasteries, the buildings gradually grow smaller and less commercial. Gradually, the river is lined with two story structures and some, even smaller.

We arrive at a small canal at a right angle to the river. It's a hot day, but while we stop to wait for the large lock that finally opens for us, we notice an increasingly oppressive heat. Even moving along the small river's increasingly uncomfortable. Happily, there are no mosquitos.

Unlike the main river, the canal has a variety of small houses, some so ramshackle they are barely standing. Many that look structurally sound have sagging roofs, look almost abandoned, except for their laundry or rugs, hanging under the eaves of the roofs. The houses are uniformly gray, and appear to be built from identical building materials. They line both sides of the canal, all with slightly pitched roofs. Most have no glass windows. We discover this is common on the canal and in the countryside outside Bangkok. Apparently, this is possible because there don't seem to be insects, and few birds either. All of this is interspersed with beautiful, perfectly manicured temples as part of the architecture of their monasteries.

It's early afternoon and after returning to the river, Linda brings the boat alongside a dock. Our boat has very low sides and the dock is somewhat higher. Even if we stand on the rear seat, those on the dock need to help us climb up onto a solid footing on the dock. Linda climbs out first with a hand from one of the men above.

Lillian is next. She manages to get up on the seat in the back of the boat, in spite of her bad leg and arthritic back and shoulders. With Linda's and my assist, we lift her legs up and roll her so that she is now horizontal on the dock. Unaware of her arthritis problem, a vicious, wiry, old woman pulls up on one of her arms. "Don't," Lillian's screaming. **"Ow! Don't do that! I can't lift my body! Let go of my arm!"**

A short, rather husky man rushes to grab her opposite arm, and also pulls. This doubles the pain. Lillian is now clearly in agony and is unable to help herself except by screaming, **"Stop, you're hurting me! Stop!"** Her cries of pain have no effect. Lillian has arthritis in her shoulders and I climb up onto the dock and have the two pulling on her arms stop.

The portion of the dock she landed on is a large, thick metal plate, and with the heat in the upper 90's, and relentless sun, the metal feels like it's on fire. It's so hot, Lillian's unable to use her hands to push up – the heat is unbearable.

I try lifting her upper body from behind to take the strain off her arms and shoulders while the short man now holds her body from the front, and the three of us get her up standing.

Even though the ordeal is very painful, she wasn't injured in the encounter.

Lillian stated "my dignity took a hit. I really was afraid my pants would catch fire!"

Linda takes us to a quick lunch at a nearby restaurant while we recount the morning adventures.

After lunch, Linda takes Lillian to visit the gem stores for which Bangkok is famous, while I return to the hotel to relax.

# 21

## *THE BEAUTIFUL ORDEAL*

THE NEXT MORNING, WE BEGIN our grand tour of the famous Buddhist temples with their Gold Buddhas. They're incredible works of art, major Buddhist religious treasures, and national treasures as well. Linda arrives at the hotel, nine o'clock sharp. She'll be our guide again.

The tour includes a large number of temples – shoes off, up the steps, pay respects (wei), enter the temple, pay respects (wei) to the Buddha, down the steps, pay respects (wei), shoes on – and on to next one, each being more incredible than the one before. The immensity of these truly beautiful gold images is unforgettable for me, but by the end of that day, we were both ready for dinner, and especially, an early bed.

On the last day, Linda meets us at a park. I've never seen so many elephants all in one place, ever. If that had occurred in another lifetime, I've totally forgotten it. For several hours, the elephants were dressed for a variety of huge, choreographed tableaus. The most memorable was an incredible warfare scene, with two armies of the elephants. Some were acting out being wounded and falling to the ground with their riders! The scene even included a large, burning castle. It was a stunning tableau.

The elephants, with their riders, re-assemble and gather at the rail facing the block long line of bleachers. They take their bows to the audience applause. Standing in the walkway between the railing and bleachers, I notice one of the twenty or thirty elephants appears slightly smaller than the others.

For me, she was a great actress, the Marlene Dietrich of the elephant world, and there was something about her that I just couldn't resist. I instantly love her. I step in close beside her with my shoulder gently pressed against her head, just in front of her ear, as if I'm going for a 'selfie" with her. I want to cuddle her, but that's out of the question. She's too big for that. So I very slowly and delicately stroke her forehead. She very lovingly and so delicately, puts her trunk around my leg and holds me with it. And much like horses that are caressed, she keeps her head there against my body. It was almost like she's purring.

We know each other, as if we had met sometime, somewhere before, and I still tear up as I think back on leaving her, even now. It's very touching to have such a large animal be so affectionate. Her rider seems very pleased with the encounter, and smiles and waves to me as they leave. Lillian is surprised. She too was touched by the scene, and she takes a photo of me stroking the elephant's forehead as it lovingly wraps its trunk around my leg. Fortunately, the elephant decided to let me go back to Lillian.

And Lillian isn't having even the teensiest bit of jealousy about my attentions to that elephant, nor of the elephant's show of affection for me. However, in spite of my next suggestion, she doesn't seem to think having a pet elephant in the back yard would be a good idea. I agree, the yard isn't big enough.

# 22

## THE CROCODILE'S PLAYGROUND

IN ANOTHER AREA OF THE same park, there's a large pool, big enough for four or five savage alligators.

It's the 'men versus alligator show'!

When hungry, the huge reptiles slink up on a sand island in the middle of the miniature lake to look for their prey. That little strip of sand is their island feeding ground. It appears their only prey at that time is a few weak looking skinny men who inhabit that island. They apparently risk their lives for a large audience of thrill seekers like me. I figure, these island guys must be the replacements for the ones that probably were eaten in the previous show.

So this huge alligator, at least four times the size of one of these skinny little men, gets hungry and slithers out of the water. It lies there playing dead. The skinny man carefully comes closer to see if it's food for him. Apparently, the alligator's still alive, and as skinny as the man is, he's the food!

Suddenly the play dead alligator moves forward and opens its jaws wide . . . very, **very wide!**

All of its teeth are showing as if it's expecting to take a bite out of an elephant . . . or gobble its skinny prey there in one bite. Mr. Skinny, or more likely, Mr. Stupid is clearly more available. Clearly – no contest!

Oops! Its jaw appears to be stuck open. I think maybe the poor beast has some kind of a defect. On second thought, I can see, the huge, vicious creature, is a reptilian mousetrap with monster teeth. I decide the crawling nightmare is challenging the skinny man to come closer to see what's inside its mouth. I can't imagine the skinny man is either that stupid, or crazy enough to take the challenge.

I was wrong. Mr. Crazy-Stupid is edging closer . . . and closer! Now, he's finally close enough to touch the nightmare's nose. I can't believe it! He's crouching down in front of the giant food grinder. I start holding my breath but I'm so nervous, I don't even feel it. Then Mr. Crazy very slowly extends his arm all the way into the alligator's huge gaping mouth, so **even his elbow's inside!** I think I'm about to faint. I can't stand to watch that puny little piece of alligator's lunch be chomped up.

The alligator just pretends its jaw is stuck, or it really could be. While I'm trying to start breathing again, I decide the skinny man must be trying to convince the alligator to go ahead and take his arm off!

Mr. Crazy's strategy must be that while the alligator is busy chewing up the tender morsel of what used to be a workable arm, Mr. Crazy, the now one-armed man, can then escape with his life. But the alligator's jaw really seems to be stuck open. So, Mr. Crazy checks this by tapping the upper inside of the monster's mouth, like 'knock, knock, who's in there . . . maybe the skinny man from the show before?'

**A loud gunshot sound!** Mr. Meat-grinder crashed his mouth shut!

It must be magic! Mr. Crazy still has his arm, complete even with fingers. Unbelievable! He's faster than the alligator can bite down. **Wow!**

He and the monster beast seem to be glaring at each other in surprise now. Then the disappointed monster turns tail and slithers back into the water. I don't get to see crocodile tears that way.

As that's happening, another alligator, even bigger than before, sneaks up on the sand and another skinnier man, comes out to try the same trick. I guess he must figure he will do something even more dangerous than his now triumphant friend, like putting his whole body inside this beast's mouth.

My heart won't take another round of this nightmare. I'm going to leave now. I stand up and head for the exit, but I can't resist and I glance back. That was a bad mistake. I'm hooked on this terrifying demonstration of insanity. I guess he decides he doesn't want to be shamed for cowardice or something like that. I definitely would have taken the shame if I were in there, and been happy to keep my arm.

Anyway, I confess that after two or three alligators go back into the water in defeat, I almost begin to feel sorry for the hungry alligators. I'm not going to try to improve their plight, however! No way!

But it does occur to me, maybe the alligators are smart enough not to bite the hand that eventually feeds them.

And I'm very proud of myself. I manage to watch the whole show without even screaming or passing out. But of course, I also kept my eyes on the alligators to make sure none of them slip under the fence with their mouths open, coming in my direction.

Lillian seems to have been fascinated by the show also. She didn't even try to leave in the middle of it.

We also attend several more shows that day including traditional Thai dancing with a dozen or so beautiful young ladies. All of them, highly accomplished and lovely dance partners. However, in spite my own popular *You Tube* performance of a modern Thai dance, I don't accept their invitation to perform with them. Our dance styles differ somewhat.

There's also the martial art of Maui Thai demonstration. The performers are very good and the techniques interest me, especially since I taught the Korean Martial Art of Tae Kwan Do in my own studio for some twenty-five years. That's when I was quite a bit younger. I miss those days now, but I still enjoy seeing such arts practiced by highly trained martial artists.

That evening, a buffet dinner precedes the stage show known as *Siam Niramit Bangkok*. It's a spectacular event performed on a vast stage with a cast of at least a hundred performers seeming to do absolutely impossible things. For example, toward the end of the show, whole groups of women in beautiful costumes seem to effortlessly float high up in space while others walk casually on the surface of what appears to be a large lake.

Nope, I'm not telling how they did it. (I confess, I don't want to look bad if I don't get it right.)

As we leave the theater after the grand finale, where large stone-like structures collapse, Lillian and I go back to our hotel to say her goodbyes. She leaves for Brooklyn the next day. We won't see each other for at least three weeks or more.

# 23

## *ENDING AND BEGINNING*

IT'S ALREADY EARLY AFTERNOON. WE'RE in the van on the six-lane elevated highway from Bangkok to the airport where Lillian will meet the Air China plane that will take her to our home in New York. Toast has chosen to come with us for the final goodbye to Lillian

In the airport, Lillian and I say our good byes as an attendant comes with the wheelchair for her. The three of us wave frantically as she disappears around the corner to the gate. It all seems too sudden.

The moment she was out of sight, Toast and I realize there is one more chance to give her a good bye at the gate. Running, we catch up with her just as she arrives in front of the entrance gate to the plane. We blow kisses and shout our good byes. Then she's out of sight and on her way back to the other world.

In all likelihood for Lillian, both of us know it's the last time she'll see Bangkok.

# 24

## AS IF

I WAKE UP AT SIX in the morning and wonder if Lillian has arrived in New York yet. Then I realize she's still somewhere in flight. I hope she's okay and getting enough sleep.

The sky is filling with the morning light. I take the elevator down to the lobby. I press the button that opens the glass doors from the elevators and stairs. As is usual, the clerks stand as I enter. We all smile as we return our greetings to one another. I go into the hotel restaurant and eat my largest meal of the day, the same breakfast I've eaten during the last two days. I'm a predictable creature of habit . . . except of course, when I'm not.

I enter the hotel dining room, and I'm astonished. The dining room is empty except for the staff. Where are the usual customers? Something must have gone wrong with the kitchen in the restaurant.

Yesterday this place buzzed with hungry people. The table with coffee and all the special additions like my wonderful croissants is gone. I get a queasy feeling in the pit of my stomach. Something's happened. I don't feel good about it.

I go to the counter and ask what happened. The head waitress smiles and says, "Oh, don't worry. Just have a seat. Your waitress will be right with you."

And, sure enough, a waitress comes to my booth with the menu. We confirm my usual order and within about five minutes, presto! The same, entire breakfast that had appeared each day, was now on the table in front of me. Amazing! It was magic again. It even includes the items I had added to my breakfast during the last week while Lillian was here. Everything from the side table with all the extras was ready for me to eat. They even know when I'll come in to eat! At that moment, I realize, when Lillian left, presto! I'm their royal guest. There's nobody else here. I can sit anywhere I choose in the whole restaurant! No one will be allowed to interfere with my choice of seating. And better yet, I'm served all the food I love!

It's like a dream. It's my private domain now, my personal dining room, complete with a devoted staff. It's the same staff we had before Lillian left. For example, I'm served the identical breakfast I ate while Lillian was here, my three croissants, fresh strawberry jam, fresh fruit, including the watermelon, juice, and my coffee.

In this moment in this place, I'm king.

This next moment I know my Queen, my Lillian has left for Brooklyn . . . I already miss her.

There will be another moment. I'm the Philosophy Professor who taught here for three years. I'm again with my fans. It's a particular moment when I've just walked out of the video, and here I am, right here with them in this great city where they live.

Wonderful!

# 25

## *JUST CURIOSITY*

KING, PROFESSOR, OR JOHN, JOHN, John, there's a paradox confronting me. As I become more acquainted with the stores and offices, I discover several puzzles.

Soon after I arrived in Bangkok, I'm in the men's room in a department store along with several other men. I notice a woman very close by, wielding a mop. Am I hallucinating? I try to pretend I didn't see her. But I watch out of the corner of my eye and see she's busy. She's paying no attention to any of us. It's as though it's her private bathroom and I'm in my private public men's room. There's a very strange part of this experience.

The other men don't notice her at all! It was like being in a men's room filled with blind men. They must be being polite, just as I am.

A week or so later, the same kind of situation occurs in a large department store men's restroom.

I finally approach Vichai. He informs me older cleaning ladies are common in the men's restrooms. I ask if that's true for men cleaning the lady's rooms. He seemed very surprised at the question. He assures me, "that could never happen. Women can't trust the men, whether young or old, in their bathrooms – just like America!"

Thinking back, I remember, soon after our arrival, Lillian and I notice our hotel bathroom floor has a drain. At first we think it makes sense. There would certainly be times when the floor could get quite wet. As we travel around in the city, we notice the same is true for department stores and restaurants.

Wherever we go, each bathroom has a drain in the center of the floor – easy to mop. We conclude this is logical, but then we realize the restaurant and department store bathrooms, without the showers, also have a drain in the floors. That seems especially unusual to us. Tile floors are common in America but most are without drains.

After a few days sightseeing in Bangkok, we realize every bathroom has one more thing in common. There's a hose with a spray nozzle connected to the same plumbing beside every toilet. We discover this is a standard fixture in every restroom including our room in the hotel. It's true, even in restaurants and department stores. We are totally baffled. Both of us had traveled to other countries in our lives, especially Lillian, and we had never seen anything quite like this anywhere else, including America.

After several extended discussions, just before Lillian left again for Brooklyn, we finally agree these fixtures must provide a very efficient way to hose down and mop the floor. We're quite sure we're right, especially since these fixtures are in all the bathrooms along with the drains. Clearly, a warm climate requires frequent cleaning, and cleanliness is essential. With that settled, we forgot all about it. Lillian was now free to leave for home.

The correct answer to that puzzle was furnished a week or so later, after Lillian had returned to Brooklyn.

# 26

## *THE NEW BEGINNING*

SIX O'CLOCK IN THE MORNING, without an alarm clock, I'm instantly alert, awake and ready for the day, whatever it will bring. It's never my regular schedule in Brooklyn unless my alarm clock stands guard to regularly dictate an hour as early as that. I attribute my amazing Bangkok schedule to fresh, nutritious Thai food, less air pollution, and the gift of a relatively stress free life of luxury. What a gift it is!

I love the Thai food, the endless variety of flavors and creativity in traditional Thai cooking. And, as I understand it, the contents are direct from the fields and gardens, as it was in my childhood.

This seems healthier than much of the food I'm used to eating in New York now. Artificial fertilizers are widely used since the end of World War One. Land is drained of natural minerals now. Most fruit and vegetables in our stores are not fresh. They've been stored in refrigeration before we get to shop for it. All kinds of sprays have been used on it to prevent insects from destroying it before harvesting. Livestock and chickens are injected with chemicals to increase their rate of growth, size, and weight. We lived in the middle of farm country and my father, as part of his veterinary practice, was providing the injections in cattle and chickens for the farmers back in the late fifties already.

In Bangkok, as I understand it, there is no need for long storage and shipping of fruit and vegetables from one continent to another. As far as I can determine, the farming uses natural organic fertilizer so the minerals were restored to the soil where food is raised. There are no preservatives, no additives, and refrigeration is often limited so fruit and vegetables are prepared on the spot. It means every dish served, is nutritious.

This shows in my complexion within the six weeks I was living in Bangkok, and is evident, even in the photographs. (My youthful appearance was commented on by nearly everyone who greeted me on my return . . . as was my level of relaxation, happiness, and good health.)

As is usual, after breakfast, a car with a staff person is waiting and finally takes me to the studio. We pull into the parking lot alongside the studio building. Parking is limited to those who work in the company buildings. Only the employees have the code for opening the doors so I'm always accompanied from the hotel to the studio by at least one employee of Salmon Publishing.

That morning, I'm led along a path between the head-high islands of thousands of packaged books, past workers doing paperwork and packaging operations. We go up several steps to a glass door and my guide presses a code box, opens the glass door, and we go up three flights on the elevator. After entering through the coded door, I'm led into a very large office space filled with desks and employees.

The moment I walk in, everyone is smiling and begins waving. I confess to tearing up as I remember this wonderful first greeting. I'm tearing up again as I write this. In America, I probably wouldn't admit my emotional state, since 'real men don't cry' in that country. However, that may be changing. I'm probably still in the Avant Garde.

After I'm introduced again to Noi, the producer, and I bow again to Benz, the person who got me here and who's in charge of every detail of my stay, and director of the creative staff. I bow then to the room filled with smiling, hand waving staff.

Next I meet Vichai again, and after the greeting formalities, he takes me to a huge room with waist high piles of books, and a large open space just inside the door.

I'm shocked.

Right in front of me, there's the exact replica of my Brooklyn office. The replica is so close in appearance to my office at home, it is still nearly impossible to tell which one I'm seeing when I look at it in a video. I congratulate the staff members who had done such a remarkable feat of duplication. My Brooklyn office space now exists on two continents half way around the world from each other.

It's amazing. Every detail is there. Even the diplomas look exactly as if they were back in my Brooklyn office. There's a metal coat rack that's a perfect replica. The parquet floor looks identical as does my chair, and the bookshelves including my haphazard papers sticking out randomly among my books.

As excited as I am, Vichai explains, "We need to prepare a few more things before we do a shoot here." As the day turns out, I have no time to be disappointed.

# 27

## *Another Challenge*

SURPRISE! THAT AFTERNOON, I'M GIVEN my first assignment. I'm to memorize, and eventually learn to sing the National military song. It begins, 'row ja tom taam son yah'. I still can hear it when I sing the first line, or rather, I pretend I can hear it. It turns out, all my life I pretended I could sing too. (I need help to keep in tune any time I even try to sing the *Happy Birthday* song I had learned at five years old.) Now anyone who hears my rendition of the Thai song knows just how badly I sing. So, 'sing' I do, and my rendition is still on *You Tube* a year later. To my astonishment, it gathered well over 500,000 viewers.

I console myself by remembering my attempt to perform a famous Thai dance. It uses the Thai steps and music of that very popular dance. My performance was seen as a parody done as a martial arts demonstration. In spite of the absurdity of my attempt to perform it, or maybe, because it is so differently performed, it attracted well over 700,000 viewers. I have Benz to thank for the three hours he spent, coaching my every movement, and capturing the results on video.

Coming into the Salmon House staff offices, even for still shots, gradually begins to feel familiar. By the time I arrive after ten in the morning, the entire staff is there, but not always. Unlike my experiences in American offices when everyone checks in and on time, except perhaps for the administrators, the Thai office seemed to be much more flexible, accepting of the worker's work load, sleep requirements, and flexible use of the office.

A few times, the entire office was completely empty, but that happens mornings after big project deadlines are met the day before. There's a fold-out couch where some of the staff sleep when they stay up too many hours. When not in use that way, the couch is my temporary 'hang-out place'. I use it for times between video shoots, appointments, socialization with staff, and my next connection with Vichai, Noi, or Benz. And as it sometimes turns out, it's the meeting place for all three plus others. It begins to feel like my new office even though I haven't used my replica of my Thai Brooklyn office yet.

As an example of the relaxed approach to appointments, one morning before I'm picked up to go to the studio, I get a message on my cell phone. "Arrive in the studio at 10:30 in the morning," so, at 10:30 I go down to the lobby. There's no car waiting yet. I find a Bangkok newspaper on a side table. It's printed in English and I comfortably plop myself down in an overstuffed chair and scan through it. Still no car. I can't concentrate on the paper and decide not to wait. I put the paper back where I found it. By this time, no car means something is definitely going wrong this morning.

As I go over to the hotel staff desk, a man wanders in and sits down in the very same leather couch where I was just sitting. He looks familiar but I can't remember his name, so I pretend I know it by saying, "oh, hello", as if I know him well.

He looks up and smiles.

I think maybe he can't remember my name either, so I continue, "your timing is great. You must be psychic,"

He replies, "Yes, I am."

I must have looked surprised. "Amazing you showed up just now,"

He continues, "I was just passing by and thought I'd check in on you."

I was even more surprised by that answer. I figure he's clearly from the studio and might possibly know my name after all. But if he really is psychic, I think he must be able to sense I need a ride. That seems the most reasonable thing to think. After all, I have several friends who are good at knowing someone else's thoughts, or name, and would even know I'm waiting for someone to come take me to the studio. I decide to continue pretending I know his name too. If he's psychic, he'll know I'm pretending. That's ok with me, and if he doesn't know that, it's even better.

But just in case he's pretending to be psychic, I explain my understanding. "I was to be at the studio at 10:30."

He says, "Oh, fine! I'll be happy to drive you over – I was just going there myself."

I say, "Great! Thank you, Mr. Psychic." I add, "I hope it's alright to call you that".

"Oh fine," he replies as we go out the door to his car. We talk all the way to the studio and he doesn't say my name and I can't remember his. It seems to work fine that way.

I look at the photo on my new cell phone when I get there and see his name is Vichai. I've already met him several times, and it's disconcerting to fail to remember him. As it turns out, he's my primary guide, driver, translator, errand runner, and all around support system for my time in Bangkok. It's embarrassing.

Even so, whenever I see him, I always think "psychic" before I say his name. I'm certain now I want to be psychic in my next life. It would actually be better to have that ability in this life, as I would have avoided picking up the food with my fingers.

So, to my delight, one of the staff takes me immediately on my second visit to the wonderful finished replica of my Brooklyn office. But it's still dark. No lighting set up, no cameras, and no one there. It looks like it does at home when I turn off the lights at midnight and call it quits.

*Damn-it*, I say to myself. I was hoping to be on the video camera that day for sure. I'm feeling let down, disappointed. What's all the stalling about, anyway? It's been two weeks since Lillian left. Back then, I expected to be on the video camera by this time. It's very puzzling since I've been told to wear my costume. My escort goes on ahead of me. She's totally oblivious of my disappointment as we leave the Bangkok replica of my Brooklyn office behind.

I follow her to the other end of the space. A photography studio's been installed there. It's complete with full lighting, a backdrop of orange paper, a desk set up with a computer with keyboard and monitor, and a grouping of chairs. In addition, off to the side, there's another table and chair where a young, well-groomed woman is seated.

Noi approaches and tells me, "you'll be on camera," but it turns out not to be the way I want. She immediately leads me to the young lady at the side table who stands up and greets me formally. She then introduces herself as my makeup artist.

She has me sit on a stool at the table. When I'm seated, Noi comes over and gives her a piece of brown and white fabric. Nothing is said between them. But before my makeup lady begins working to prepare my face for the lights and the camera, she carefully removes my usual blue neck tie, and gently replaces it with a new necktie. It looks like it's made of giraffe hide, except its fabric.

Strangely, I've never gotten feedback on that tie. It occurs to me, it might appear I had been on a safari, and this is the remains of my trophy? (Do they eat giraffe meat?) I would never shoot a giraffe. Even if I did kill it by accident somehow, I'd be too embarrassed to admit it in either case.

I spend several hours being gussied up for what appears to be an upcoming photo shoot. The details include eye shadow, my hair is treated and combed, and even my bushy white eyebrows are trimmed to 'thin perfection'. After what feels like hours of work to fix me up enough to be on camera, I'm declared ready for the shoot. At least lipstick isn't on the menu, to my relief.

The camera and light set up is in place, and by that time, the gathering of staff includes more than a dozen members including the Publicity and Marketing Directors, as well as the lighting person, and camera man.

This puzzling behavior is suddenly very clear. I'm sent into the orange set for the photo shoot. The lights are turned on, and a person comes on stage and carefully places me where I'm to stand. Another person comes out to adjust my jacket and I'm directed to take a pose. The camera makes some clicking sounds, and then, another pose with a change of facial expression, followed by moving my hands, arms, head, eyes, and on it goes.

After more than an hour, the lights are turned down and a small group of directors and technicians gather around a television screen to the side of the work area. Noi arrives to rescue me with a fresh hot cup of coffee. As I gulp it down, she suggests, "It might be a good time for you to sit down and take a break."

"I'm for that." I respond and head for an empty chair with another gulp of coffee.

Meanwhile the techies and directors make their choices of which shots they want. As I find out, they are also making choices for those specific projects they are each responsible for or, are producing.

When I return from my coffee break, the lights were turned on and the camera man takes his post behind the camera. The next series of shots are poses that suggest action of all kinds, from martial arts poses to dance moves, varied facial expressions, some of which I think would be appropriate for Halloween, or a demented monster movie. I assume some of them would never even be used. As it turns out, I guessed wrong. While not everything is published, everything is "grist for the mill," to quote an old saying.

What's all this about? I have no idea at the time. I decide that as long as they put me on camera, they're up to something. After all, I'm not here to figure it out. All I have to do, is to do as they ask. It seemed to work every time . . . so far.

A few days later, one reason for the shoot was made clear. This is preparation for the introduction of a new, oversize Magazine to be called *Giraffe*. One of my still shots is to be used for the cover. Others are featured inside along with a text about me. The plan is to distribute it free in the subway system as one way to create public awareness of the new series of videos where I'm to be featured. With that news, I'm beginning to feel hope. I'll be on camera in my 'twin' office after all.

Within two days, the graphic design group is working late and churning out pages. Whenever I come into the office, advertising is being planned along with the copy that has already been written. It is all pinned up on the wall until it's approved. And a day later when Vichai brings me back to the studio, there I am already on at least four mockups for the cover. Either that or they're planning four editions of the magazine featuring me. I'm for that!

Then I finally notice, the photo where my usual costume necktie has been replaced is pinned up. It's put first along with the other shots. My imaginary trophy from my imaginary safari takes its place.

Impossible! This is crazy. It's too **extreme – the end of the tie is**

**dangling from my mouth?** I look like a slow-motion vomit of my dead giraffe dinner, as if I hunt giraffes for my dinner.

I don't give my opinion to anyone, but I desperately hope the picture would be rejected. So, of course, it's the one chosen to fill the mammoth cover! By mammoth cover I mean sixteen inches high and almost a foot wide.

I just don't understand. I decide to keep quiet and trust the staff to know what they're doing. Maybe there's some special meaning everyone in Bangkok knows except for me.

About a week later, the oversize first issue of *Giraffe* is printed and distributed free on the two subway lines. I'm not sure how many issues, if any, landed in the hands of my followers, but I soon found out. The oversize image of me vomiting the skin of my trophy drew thousands and thousands of followers who crowded into the National Book Fair carrying copies of *Giraffe* for me to sign. I just don't understand the process of promotion.

# 28

## *AND OH FOR SOME IMPROVISATION*

**FINALLY!** THE DAY I WAITED for! **Hooray!**

I enter the replica of my Brooklyn office in Bangkok! Lights! Position! Camera! I'm finally ON! (Wrong. Very Wrong.)

It's my first day in the studio and I find out it takes most of the morning to arrange my chair in the right place.

"Easy," you say?

The arrangement includes locating the exact correct position for the chair, the chair relative to the monitor, the chair relative to the camera, the teleprompter, and my microphone. Everything is related to me, and as I find out that day clearly, everything in the system has to be related to everything else – and precisely positioned.

For example, I sit in the same identical place in the set, whether in Brooklyn, or Bangkok. There are little L shaped marks on the floor to designate the four wheels on the four legs of my chair. These L shaped marks are moved when my chair is moved. One of the 'tech' staff carefully adjusts my chair. All I have to do is sit still . . . and continue sitting still . . . and more sitting still, as the camera is moved a few inches or less, focused, moved, and re-focused, then the chair is moved and finally, the little squares moved.

Each time, the image in the camera registers in the video monitor where Benz was stationed. The image has to be centered in the monitor. He sees what the camera sees, including even my slight eye moments. If the image in the monitor isn't placed right, the camera and/or my chair is shifted slightly. Until all the variables are lined up perfectly, the process is repeated. Fortunately, I don't have any problem with motion sickness, and I had enough sleep. I broke the pattern occasionally with bathroom trips. No, that wasn't videoed, (as far as I know as I write this).

Then the lights are adjusted. One light is placed inside the replica of the office while two, and sometimes three others, are posted to the side with slightly different angles. These have to be brought closer, moved, checked again and so on, and on, until all the lights are properly placed. And if you think this description is boring, it's only a glimpse of that morning.

The microphone is next. No, it's not in front of me because I'm not going to stand up to sing, or lecture. This need to be a very tiny microphone because it's never to appear on camera, ever. A sound technician has the dismal task of keeping it perfectly invisible. But it isn't so simple. It has to be placed to pick up my voice, and not the sound of my breathing, or my shirt moving as I breathe, but at the same time it can't be seen!

I have a small fabric container, with a zipper, fastened to my belt outside on my right side. It holds my cell phone. It turns out to be perfect for the little microphone amplifier that's electronically included with the video shot. So, I evict my cell phone to make a place for the amplifier.

Now it all gets a little more personal. To install the microphone on my body, requires a rather long cord running from the amplifier to the tiny little bump on the end of that cord that functions as a microphone. It has a miniature clip on it. It's my duty to stuff all that endless cord (it feels like at least 20 feet but is only about 5 or 6 feet) up inside my pants. Then, it has to come up under my shirt and come out just under the knot in my necktie.

When it finally arrives there, the sound tech then attempts to clip it to my shirt, just under the knot in my tie, if he doesn't strangle me in the process. This setup is tested as I babble nonsense, my favorite nursery rhyme, "Mary had a little lamb, its fleece," etc., until the right volume and clarity is approved by Benz.

When the "mike" as it's called, is clear and free of the sound of my shirt or necktie rubbing against it, (and has not short circuited somewhere in the cord or mike) we're ready for the next step. Until I become used to its location, it tangles in my underwear whenever I visit the men's room.

I confess, memorizing more than one line at a time becomes a challenge, especially when it contains Thai words in it. While I did memorize a series of curse words for the video done in Brooklyn with Benz, it couldn't work that way this time because it would require too many takes.

The tech staff was now pressured to find a way to feed my lines to me without making it look like I'm reading a teleprompter. My teleprompter sits on the table very slightly to my right. As seen from where I'm seated, I need to be able to see the text without looking away from the camera. To do this, the teleprompter has to be close enough to me to read it easily without my glasses, and without moving my eyes back and forth.

When that finally is working, there's the necessity of having me talk in sentences. Being able to recite as many as eight or nine sentences was often a requirement because of the difference in the delivery required to sound spontaneous. In that case it requires the operator of the teleprompter to be able to adjust the size, boldness, space between lines, background color, text color, and number of lines that can be done at one take, so that I can read them. The teleprompter operator has a cruel and inhuman job, but as they say, "someone has to do it."

A young lady named Annya is operator of the teleprompter. As we begin shooting the scenes, I have a problem I can't control. It isn't her fault. My eyes flicker quick eye movements in her direction. She even turns away while I'm doing my lines. I just can't help it. I can't feel myself do it. She is attractive, and certainly, I like her, but the problem isn't that. We don't know that however.

Several on the staff seem to feel I would do better with an ophthalmologist and lenses, but there isn't time to send me to one. I think there's even a quiet suggestion that I might do even better with a Psychologist or Psychotherapist. Vichai was put in her place. Same problem. My eyes keep suddenly flickering in his direction while I was saying my lines. He too, turns away and finally moves completely out of sight. That works, and the shoot goes on.

Besides that particular difficulty, continually adjusting the teleprompter for me turns out to be the source of much continuing work, and frustration, even for Vichai. In fact, this problem is only solved after nearly a week of shooting. The teleprompter is finally positioned so I can read and say three lines spontaneously.

As the weeks go on, another problem presents itself on camera. I'm gaining weight! – resulting in poor posture. The seat of the chair tilts back slightly. Because of my increasing stomach bulge, the slightest slouch increases the visual problem. That can't be remedied by changing the chair because it's the only chair that resembles the one in my Brooklyn office. I don't have a girdle either. That means I have to sit up straight. In that position, my back is no longer supported because of the chair tilt. I find I need to hang onto the chair seat in front to get into a truly straight posture. I hold onto it for dear life for the length of time it requires to get a final take. I still perspire thinking about it.

Benz seems to be in charge of my posture as well as my eye movements, intonation, volume, amount of energy required for the line, whether I'm too much the professor, or not enough; whether I'm too "Broadway," and so on. Then, as I get the line right and think I can relax just a little, I hear another, "**straighten up!**" Then we start again. By then, I have to re-read the teleprompter to get my line right.

I straighten up by pulling myself up in place. Then the person who has the clapboard approaches. Benz says, "Ready!" It isn't a question, it's a way to alert me the shot is to begin shortly, and then, CLACK! The clapboard indicates we're on camera, and it's another take. No sagging now.

A short sequence of Thai words, along with the rest of the sentence in English, was the most difficult for me. There's always a pronunciation session while I find a way to say each word, and then find a way to integrate it into the whole sentence, as if I said it naturally all my life. Apparently, I speak the language well enough to convince listeners I had actually been a professor of philosophy, teaching in Thailand for three years.

In my experience, no one has ever derisively asked, "why don't you just do the whole show in English?"

# 29

## *OOPS!*

A WEEK OR SO INTO the shoot, I go into the men's room and notice, there's no toilet paper.

So, uncomfortable though I am, I pull up my pants, wire and all, and look in the next stall. No luck. No toilet paper in the next one either.

I nervously check the door on the women's restroom. It's dark. I check in each stall, and damn it! No luck there either. By this time, I'm desperate. I finally find several tissues in my pocket and relieve myself in the men's room.

When I go back into the camera area, I tell Noi and the others, "There's no toilet paper in either the men's or ladies room." They don't seem to be particularly concerned . . . or more likely; their silence indicates I'm mentioning something very private in a mixed audience.

However, at this time, I don't think of that. I just think they seem puzzled by my comments or possibly, concerned that I will continue to create an uncomfortable situation. Whatever it is, they seem anxious to get on with the shoot. I decide they must all carry their own tissues, so I make sure I'm well supplied the next day. When I check the men's room the next day, toilet paper is in place.

A few days later, I'm sitting on the couch in the work area, and Vichai sits down beside me. We start talking about the shoot that day. When there's a pause I ask Vichai, "why isn't there any toilet paper in the rest room, and what accounted for no one being concerned?"

He thinks for a moment and says, "well, with the hose beside the toilet to clean up with, it isn't really all that important. Toilet paper's sometimes used for a quick dry up."

I burst out laughing and reply, "Lillian and I thought the hose was for cleaning the bathroom floors."

After we both have a good laugh, he explains, "from childhood, the children are all taught to use the hoses."

I notice however, toilet paper is always in the toilet stalls after that.

When I return to the hotel that evening, I decide, this evening is as good a time as any to perfect my skill, just in case. After all, if young school children can make this thing work, certainly I should be able to master it with no difficulty. Just to play it safe, I'll do a trial run.

I position myself on the toilet, ready for action.

Very cautiously, I take the menacing contraption from its attachment on the wall and point it carefully toward the floor drain just to get used to the nozzle. I press the handle. There's an explosion of water. I decide I pressed too hard on the trigger and I'll take it easier this time.

I position the nozzle near the intended target under me with my right hand. I realize I'm not sure just exactly where the intended target might be. I'm very nervous, now. It's like pulling the fire alarm in school during classes to see what will happen next.

I check my position as best I can . . . squeeze! Water explodes from between my legs – on the floor, wall, towels – as I rectify my aim, it's all over; my behind – bathtub, shower curtain, floor – pant legs, shoes, face . . . I give up!

Knowing I can't even do as well as a three-year-old, I decide I better stop for the evening. I've done enough cleanup already.

However, I can be foolishly stubborn. I have plans to go back to solving the problem tomorrow. I certainly should be able master a hose with water in it. But I do understand why there's a drain in every bathroom floor in Bangkok. It's there in case a beginner comes in. Or worst of all, an old adult from America comes in and desperately tries to use it for the first time.

# 30

## *NO SHORT CUTS*

IT'S THE NEXT DAY. I'VE just finished my breakfast that morning. My driver arrives and I'm driven to the studio and I'm told we are going to a shoot on-site. It's a monastery some distance from Bangkok.

I remember, a small group of us gathers out by the street to wait for our van. When it arrives, we climb in with the video team, the tech people, lighting group, and all the equipment. We're to go on-site for a scene with an actor who always plays the part of a monk.

It's in the nineties and I'm dressed in my usual formal attire with my winter sport jacket over my shirt and tie. I sit in the seats behind the driver and Noi, tucked in between Vichai on one side of me and Benz on the other.

We gradually leave the commercial buildings as we enter a layered tangle of express highways beside us, and even above us. We stay on those that are mostly local. It seems like the trip goes for several hours that day, although it could be less. It's an interesting ride. It only seems long.

We finally end in an area of low buildings and more open space, where we finally drive past the gates of a major monastery and into a large courtyard. The van drives up to a building, where we bail out, stretch, and begin to get our legs working again.

The crew hauls their equipment out of the van and piles it up in an open space under the monastery building. Out of respect, we all take our shoes off as we enter the space under the building, even the crew.

The tech people haul the equipment up a flight of stairs to the next floor for the shoot.

It's very humid, and in the nineties. There's no relief, even in the shade under the building above us. Since I'm in my costume, thankfully, Noi suggests, "Stay downstairs here. You might as well enjoy the occasional slight breeze here in the shade of the building. The set-up will be slow upstairs."

As she turns to go back up, she introduces me to my acting partner. He's a man who played the role of a monk for many years in Thai movies. Then she returned to the upstairs.

My acting partner and I wait under the shade of the building. I can't speak Thai and he isn't much better with English. Perhaps because of this, he and I get along quite well. I relax while he works on memorizing his lines.

It's been two hours of travel time. As usual, I discover I need a restroom. I'm not sure where to find such a facility. Noi and the others are upstairs preparing the space for the 'on camera' part of our visit. Since my acting partner spoke no English, I asked one of the priests wandering past. He's apparently sworn to silence and points to the closed door just besides the stairs to the second floor. I gratefully go in.

"Yikes!" There's no toilet! It's just a hole in the floor.

I leave and close the door. I consider finding a large tree. However, it's not that simple, partly because there's quite a population of wandering monks, and also, I won't be making such a simple visit.

In desperation, I re-open the door, and go back inside. Then, in the somewhat dim light, I see there's a ceramic structure set into the floor. It looks much like a shallow ceramic bowl with a hole in the bottom. I realize it's a fancy version of a more primitive facility, (if you're lucky) available in India, and most other Asian countries. I'm told it is often only a simple hole in the ground. Lillian had described her adventures with this form of facility in her travels through India, China, and all the way into Tibet.

It's becoming urgent, and I'm increasingly nervous. I realize I have to maintain a squatting position over the thing long enough to meet my needs. And there it is, the one-eyed wonder, staring back at me. It looks like a leftover porcelain wash tub that's recycled because of the gaping hole in the bottom.

I have no choice but to try to make it work ok. It does test my balance and my stamina. In spite of my age, I manage without losing my balance even though there's nothing to hang onto. And I struggle to get up without falling over . . . or in! I doubt if anyone would come to my rescue.

I realize, they couldn't get the door open. I had made sure I locked the door from the inside.

With great effort, I do manage. However, because it's not a toilet, there's no hose beside it. Bummer! No toilet paper either! Double bummer!

I've managed so far, but I'm increasingly desperate . . . I've used all of the small supply of paper in my pocket from the day before. I took it for granted all monasteries have toilet paper. I finally spot a small, stone-walled structure next to my porcelain wash tub. The structure is partially filled with water. It has a bowl sitting on top of the low wall. I just manage to reach it. It's hardly a perfect answer, but I make do.

I come out and wait outside, hoping the heat will help dry me off. I'm still a little more than damp yet when I'm called to work with my acting partner. He's now dressed in his tan robes. I notice they aren't the deep traditional color of the robes in the monastery, but apparently, the different color went unnoticed in his many movies.

We're shown to the room with the book-like materials used by the monks. The materials are used when a person pays the monk to have their name changed. It's a time-honored method to bring them good luck.

He and I both sit cross legged on the floor. I had practiced sitting that way during meditation for many years, but as we sit facing each other, I quickly discover time has taken a toll. This position is quickly becoming painful. I manage at first, in spite of my ankles that are still attempting to recover from the open wounds. The right ankle was not healed yet and it's the one I have to tuck under in a cross legged position. Gradually, it becomes painfully distracting.

I hope the shoot will be short. I have very few lines.

Wrong. I'm the <u>only</u> one with very few lines. My acting partner, poor fellow, has very many lines and we have to do the whole thing over and over, take after take. Being damp is nothing compared with sitting with my legs crossed for what seems like *forever*. It's torture but I do my best not to fidget or show pain.

My hours sitting during Buddhist practices turns out to be very useful. In any case, my acting partner and I manage to give me a new Thai name in the process. Since he isn't a real priest anyway, I've reverted to my ordained name. I've had continuing good luck with that one.

# 31

## *ARTISTIC GLORY*

IT'S A HOT, GRAY, STICKY-HUMID morning here in Bangkok. I'm called to go on site for a shoot in my usual costume – tie and jacket – appropriate for the cool fall weather in New York. I notice the temperature is above ninety. As usual, I have no idea what I'll be doing, but I do know the shoot is on site somewhere. We're stuffed together in the van, Noi in the front seat, Benz, Vichai and I in the next seat, (me in the middle between the two of them just in case I would try to escape?) and behind us, the crew is stuffed in under, and on top of their piles of equipment.

After the two-hour scenic view of the Bangkok's 'outer communities' and no air-conditioning, we arrive at the site where the shoot is scheduled. My jacket already looks like it's just been in a torrential rain storm.

We pull up alongside a multi-story residential building. Surprise. There's a light tan wall covered with half a city block of large graffiti . . . or so it appears at first. I guess it must have been created by a giant with a love of scribbling. I picture him, or more probably her, brandishing a ten-foot-long lipstick, endowed with a bright pink color. I knew right away it was my fate to admire this defilement of a residential building. It's as if it's an historical treasure of high art, left for several centuries by none other than Leonardo Di Vinci himself . . . or more likely, his wife. I decide to keep my opinions to myself.

We manage to untangle ourselves and stumble out of the van. I notice a person standing near the wall. Noi and Vichai introduce us. He'll be on camera with me. Since I have very few lines for this shoot also, I guess he must have a lot of lines or else we just walk admiringly back and forth in front of the graffiti. Anyway, he isn't practicing lines and seems not to pay much attention to the wall either. For the shoot, I decide I need to *pretend* to be impressed. I'm acting, after all. I've been spoiled by the vast display of creative graffiti that covered most of the New York City subway cars, stations, and even a sky scraper or two. That was at least twenty years ago. It covered nearly all the thousand subway cars, the underside of the highway overpasses, and whole sides of many of the hundreds of thousands of buildings, large and small. In fact, as this wonderful (and too short lived) artistic movement gained momentum, the hardware stores began running short of spray can colors. Often, the artists of that time ran out of money to buy the colors they needed, so a portrait face might end up green with blue hair or lipstick pink. It was truly wonderful!

It was a joy to walk around the different areas of New York, or just sit in the subway watching the wonderful moving art show going by on the subway cars and the buildings when we emerged from the tunnels. For me, it was preferable by far to going to the tourist sites such as Central Park or the Empire State Building. That was before the wretched, and even despicable cleanup of the graffiti. Since most of it has been removed and forbidden, there are still good remains of it in Brooklyn, and a touch of it going north along the Hudson River beside the railroad tracks.

# 32

## *LUNCH TIME*

THIS PARTICULAR DAY, ONE MAN with remarkably better than 20/20 eyesight comes down from something like the 10th floor prior to the shoot. He wants a selfie with **me.** He requests the two of us take our pose as if we are in the process of cursing. He hurries back with his treasure the moment we finish the shot.

Otherwise, the video shoot is rather routine, with many takes. The actor who has all the lines this time, paces back and forth while I pace back and forth, both of us pretending to admire the genius of the anonymous artist. He gives a long speech about graffiti and we pace back and forth on camera some more. All the while, I'm getting really hungry. Finally, by the time we finish, it's mid-afternoon. We all agree, there's still time for late lunch.

The crew stuffs all the gear, item by item, back into the van. By then I'm ready to suck the sweat out of my tie to replenish my dehydration and salt deficiency. I don't have my giraffe skin tie which would seem more appropriate. Finally, the crew begins packing themselves on and into the collection of cameras, iPods, cables, etc., all of which is delaying my intense need to gratify my increasingly intense thirst and starvation syndrome.

We're finally all jammed in place and travel a short distance on a main road. I was giving up on any prospect of my survival. To my surprise, there are suddenly 'open front' food shops the whole length down the street as far as I can see. To my relief, the van stops in the middle of this promising gustatory array.

A wall of cars and vans are parked bumper to bumper along both sides of the road as far as I can see. I confess, I'm very encouraged to have so many people flocking to the restaurants. They must be an absolutely super place to have been chosen by so many, especially at this time of day!

I'm the last one onto the tarmac. I'm feeling stiff, tired, half starved, and very thirsty, so I walk more slowly than the others. Most seem to have gained quite a lead on me. I assume that is probably because of their greater survival instincts due to food and water deprivation.

As I struggle on in my weakened condition, I feel a few very tiny raindrops and notice the clouds are getting darker. No problem. It doesn't look serious. I notice more of the crew are passing me, but as I'm continuing to stumble along toward the place that has been chosen, someone behind me shouts, **RUN!** Bodies race past. Then I feel heavier drops of rain. Are all my friends going crazy? They must be even hungrier than I am. Maybe it's a foot race? They're not – WHOOSH – buckets of water full in the face! Blinding! I'm totally drenched. It's a wall of water, all of it on my outside.

I'm still thirsty, and my tie is a now sodden mess as it sticks to my shirt. I want to suck on it but I find myself blinded, running now, bumping into cars and hearing voices shouting. **"Here!" "Here!"** I try to get to the voices and turn between two parked cars. I suddenly find myself in an open restaurant. I try to wipe my eyes to see but my hands just put more water in my eyes. I try with my sleeve but it's so wet I make it worse. As I stand there dripping, I finally begin to see people sitting there. They all look like strangers.

I don't see anyone I know.

Someone to my left is still repeating, **"HERE," "HERE!"** I feel someone take my arm and lead me into the next open front restaurant. Everyone is laughing, and they make room for me to sit down.

They've nearly finished eating. My food arrives and I wolf it down. Then, as I'm stuffing food in my mouth as fast as I can. I look around for a moment while I come up for air. Everyone's disappeared!

Still chewing the last few bites, I desperately run along the road past the parade of parked cars. I'm getting out of breath and I hear a horn beep behind me. The van driver had seen me pass and was now speeding along right behind me. I would have appreciated an earlier beep.

# 33

# *KO MAN THAI*

IT'S NOW WELL INTO MY stay. We're still working on the episode where I search for the perfect dish of *Ko Man Thai*. I have to confess, I found other dishes in the time I was in Bangkok that I liked better. However, I had learned my script. It was very short. I had only to say my order to the waitress.

However, like all shoots, it requires Noi, the camera people, lighting techs, sound techs, Benz, and Vichai. All are required, plus an actress playing the part of the waitress, and myself. In this scene, the set had to be a restaurant and the one chosen was about two blocks from the studio.

It was popular. It was usually well attended, even becoming very crowded on some occasions. We'd gone there sometimes for lunch and fairly often for our evening meals. It was a small open front place with sky blue walls and a variety of good Thai cooking.

An arrangement was made with the place to do our shoot there. The setup of cameras and lighting has already preceded the actress. A table in the far corner is reserved for me. The shoot occupies more than a quarter of the total space because of the camera, lights, and technical crew. By the time the filming is ready, the restaurant's packed to more than full capacity.

I remain sitting while lighting is arranged and re-arranged. The volume of conversation has come to the level of the traffic outside, or even more. My actress/waitress finally arrives to take my order.

With the huge shoulder to shoulder crowd all talking at once, I can barely hear Benz shout, **"Ready – Action!"** I can't hear the usual clap of the wooden boards but the actress is already standing near me. She comes close with her order pad and pen, bends toward me and asks, "Can I take your order?"

I actually can't hear what she said, but I proceed to place my order in English. It's my memorized script. My actress/waitress appears to make a note in her book. I think I hear a faint **"Cut,"** but I'm not sure since the crowd is so loud it's very hard to hear.

One of the tech people edges through the crowd with the message to **"talk louder!"**

I remain seated at my table while the waitress goes back to her place a short distance into the crowd. I'm not sure, but I think I hear **"ready – action!"**

The crowd noise is super loud, like an auditory fog that covers any words, even when shouted. The actress has already struggled her way through to me, so I give my order, or rather, shout my order again.

The camera man comes over to me and shouts, **"talk even louder!"**

I want to shout back at him, **"I AM TALKING LOUDER,"** but he's already swallowed up in the crowded, already overstuffed restaurant. I'm sure nobody hears me anymore above the continuing ROAR. Apparently, the only cue is the actress approaching me. I try to be heard during several more attempted takes. The room gets even noisier. I can't hear anything she's saying.

I sit waiting. My waitress doesn't come back again. I think maybe she simply walked out in despair. I continue to sit . . . waiting. I can't see any staff either. I know I'll lose my seat and the table if I get up to go find out what's going on with the shoot. Either the restaurant will eventually empty out enough for someone from the shoot to come get me. If that doesn't happen, I know how to walk the two blocks back to the studio.

Come to think of it, I wouldn't be able to get in, since I don't know the code to open the door and the staff at the front entrance has already left. However, they've never abandoned me yet. I watch the crowd, satiated with talk and food, gradually spreading out into the street. The front of the place is wide open.

Finally – here he comes – emerging from the quieting uproar – the camera man – the only remaining member of the crew! He signals me to leave as he finishes his final packing. I follow him back the two blocks to the studio.

I go sit on my couch. I hear no more about the waitress scene until the middle of my last week in Bangkok.

# 34

## *HARD TO CHOOSE*

AS I RECALL, VICHAI PLANS on taking me to shop for a backpack as requested by Lillian. We're out by the street, where there's the usual, very heavy traffic. He just holds up his hand and a fellow on a motorcycle, wearing the red-orange taxi jacket, (and no helmet) pulls up in front of me. (When driving a motorcycle, it's the law to have a helmet on in America, and there are no motorcycle taxis either, unfortunately.)

In a moment, another motorcycle taxi magically appears in front of Vichai. Apparently, they're psychic too. He says something in Thai to the driver, and to me he says in English, "get on." I'm not as agile as I used to be, and after a struggle, I get my leg up over the back of the machine and manage to get seated. In spite of my success, my feet are still dangling down.

I hear Vichai shout, **"feet on foot rests!"** My feet find the foot rests as I fumble for the handholds. We're already in high gear as I find the hand holds are down behind me. It feels like zero to eighty miles an hour in one second.

It's breathtaking – as we zoom around people – between cars – careen to the edge of the road – back to the center – and it's back to the edge – turn a corner nearly lying down on our side. I'm sure I'll land in the street careening around every corner. Then – speed bumps – and we're airborne. I close my eyes. I'm sure we sailed over the top of at least one car – another wicked curve – and everything stops.

I open my eyes. We're there. I stagger off the two-wheel monster as if I had just finished a bottle of Saki. As I continue staggering around in my efforts to avoid falling down, I stammer, for Vichai's benefit, **"wow, that was fun!"**

I see Vichai is casually climbing off his motorcycle with the grace of a modern dancer. Vichai is so polite. He just nods.

And how did he manage to get there first anyway? I decide he must have been airborne over me on a speed bump while my eyes were closed. Of course, since he's psychic, so he can probably bi-locate or something like that.

Anyway, in my case, I consider myself lucky to have gotten there at all.

As my normal vision returns, sort of, I find we're at the subway station again, where the two subways meet. When I manage to catch my breath, and begin to walk, I decide it actually has been very exciting and fun . . . well, enough fun so I did manage to go back to the hotel on another motorcycle taxi after our shopping trip.

I did it without falling off mid-way, or even throwing up, passing out, or anything.

I knew I could get used to it . . . eventually.

# 35

## *HALLUCINATION, I HOPE*

ONE DAY, I'M BEING FOLLOWED. Well, not quite followed – I'm attracting attention. It sounds like some kind of a bird repeating itself, over and over – a combination hybrid rooster and loudspeaker becoming louder – and **louder** – its call increasingly eerie.

**Kakaouh** (pronounced **Kakaaoouu**, or something like that).

After a week or so, it finds my room on the eighth floor. Each day, somewhere nearby, it starts its very loud call, becoming louder and closer, as well as more eerie.

**Kakaouh,** (pause) **Kakaouh,** (pause) **Kakaouh.** I can't sleep with that damn racket, even if I wanted to. I'm very curious. I want it to go away, but I also want to see what the creature looks like.

One morning, I think I finally have my wish. It's right there on my balcony. So I think, ah-HA! I'll catch sight of the thing right **now!** I leap out of bed, race out onto my balcony stark naked to surprise it. Whatever it is. I figure it will be so shocked and embarrassed, it will never return.

It isn't there! The balcony is totally empty. No souvenir. Not even a stinky little dropping, or a feather. No sound of flapping wings either. I look on the ledge that runs along the building. No bird. Nothing. I'm so upset! I shout "*%#*&~*#! **bird!**" I shout that word at it and it stays quiet. I'm thinking maybe the damn bird or whatever it is understands English swear words.

Just my wishful thinking, and no such luck.

That bird creeps up again in another neighborhood soon after the sneak attack at the hotel. If it's a real person, I'd complain to the hotel to "Get rid of him, it, her, them" to start with. But this way, it stays invisible, like a ghost.

So, a few days later four or five of us are walking back from a shoot nearby. We come to a little platform with a cyclist asleep with his motorcycle beside him. Noi decides she wants a few still shots in case they would be good for publicity. She wakes the motorcyclist up and gets his permission to use his motorcycle as a prop for the photo. He agrees and even loans me his red-orange jacket for added authenticity.

I'm sitting on the motorcycle taxi wearing the red-orange jacket, reading a paper. Meanwhile the owner of the motorcycle sprawls out for another wink or two of his mid-day nap.

Unbeknownst to me, the bird stays hidden high up in a nearby tree, carefully watching me. Suddenly, I hear **Kakaouh!** It's a shock – really loud right near me. I look around. I can't see it.

The bird was loud enough again, so the motorcycle owner wakes up. I ask him, "what kind of bird is it? Maybe it's yours?" the bird hollers right in the tree above us. He looks up and shouts his own obscenity . . .

"#*(>%<~T##*. That thing sure isn't mine. It makes too much noise!" I agree.

I say, "I'll try starting the motorcycle. That'll scare it!"

No luck. I think it was Noi who photographed me pointing in the direction I want to go to escape the bird or ghost, or whatever the crazy invisible thing is. I realize, of course, I can't do that. It's not my motorcycle.

But just at that moment, all is silent again. It's deliberately staying out of sight. I get off the motorcycle to see if I can see it. Noi with the *Salmon Studio* group and I, move around looking up at the top of a tall tree where the sound seems to come from. Try as we can to see it, no luck!

I feel uneasy as we go back to the studio. I don't want that crazy ghost bird following me there too.

For more than a week, I don't hear it again. I assure myself, it's given up at last. I even stop looking around nervously to be sure it won't show up again. But then, one late afternoon in the studio, we're almost finished with the shoot. I'm on camera practicing the three lines for the next take. As we go on camera and I'm almost done with the second line. The crazy ghost bird is suddenly screaming **Kakaouh** at me just as I'm starting my third line.

Benz shouts – **"Stop,"**

The wretched bird is lurking close by, right outside the studio. It screams again, very loud.

We all wait. The bird stops.

We're on! **"Action!"** I finish two lines. I'm starting my third line again. The cursed beast screams at me again.

Benz shouts – **"Stop!"**

The take is ruined again. Silence, and once more, we begin. And again, screaming. Ruined again.

No matter how long we wait, the crazy ghost bird (as I call it) screams at me. It reminds me of my mother, screaming **"Nelson!" "Nelson!" "Nelson!"** But she is dead – gone for years! She didn't want me to be an actor, or an artist. Or, it could be my ex getting even with me for leaving? There's no point in trying to figure it out, whatever it is, it's unforgettable.

I can't stand it. I scream, "*%#*&~)*#!, get away from me! **Never come back!**"

We all start screaming, "**Never come back!**" "**Never come back!**" "**Never come back!**"

There is a strange thing about all this. After the third day when we all screamed at the creature, it never returned to the studio to interrupt a shoot. It's never followed me to Brooklyn either.

I confess, I sort of miss it in the morning, sometimes. And I'm sorry if I yelled like that at my mother, if that was her coming back to be with me. And I'm also sorry I yelled at my ex, if it was she instead. I'll probably have to pay for this in my next life . . . even if it <u>was</u> just a bird . . . or a ghost.

# 36

## *NOVEMBER 14, 2001*

FINALLY, TODAY'S **THE THAI NATIONAL Book Fair!**

I can't resist a **Hooray!**

Benz, and I, and a van load of us have arrived at the Fair. We pass groups of people milling around in the hall near the refreshment center. It's a small part of an enormous lounge area, and as we're walking toward another area with walls of people, gathering in a large opening in the building. I can only guess we'll be entering it next.

Noi and Benz both told me, "thousands are here to have you sign their books. Now that I'm here, I'm so excited, it seems unreal. I didn't even write the books! Benz did! I don't know what he said about me in those books either. They're written in Thai, but whatever it is, it must be really good! I can hardly think. Thousands and I'm only in one chapter in each book but there are huge lines of people who aren't even in the hall with us yet.

We're moving slowly with so many people. I'm feeling impatient and nervous at the same time. Four people from Salmon House move closer to us, forming a circle around us. Benz advises me, "We'll need to stay in close together now." I feel more calm; I don't feel so alone.

I notice others from the bus following closely as we approach the room for the signing. There's a mammoth crowd milling in the entry way ahead of us. We aren't even in the entry way yet. It looks overwhelming.

When we get to the entrance, the hall is a vast sea of people, so packed in, there's no room to move. As we come closer, this huge ocean begins to part, just enough for us to continue forward. We continue walking into it, like the vast sea opening one step at a time while it closes behind us. I've never seen anything like this. It doesn't seem real, but I'm a part of it too. Amazing.

Our circle is becoming like a cage now. It's grown to six people surrounding Benz and I. It's as if we're in a submarine with periscopes seeing the sea of faces we are moving through. I'm simply part of our boat.

I've performed for large audiences, but never quite like this. Never entered into the midst of an audience who already seems so intently focused on me in this way. It's so strange, passing through this nearly silent ocean of people step by step, so steadily, and so quietly. There is no cheering, no waving to us, no selfies, and no jostling for a better look.

I guess I was expecting the kind of excitement that went with college football crowds when I was much younger. The moment the players appear, everyone begins pushing and cheering, even screaming as the uniforms are seen, numbers recognized, and a kind of madness takes over. It feels very different here, as if each person in our presence is soaking us in, absorbing our inner being, and cherishing the feeling of doing that.

As we slowly drift to the center of the room, I finally see a raised white table and two chairs. I'm reminded of an island with a lighthouse.

As we approach it, several of our people have already arrived ahead of us. When I climb up onto a low platform, I'm told to sit on the chair to the right. Also, the four of our group forming a barrier around Benz and me, now are posted around our miniature office. In our two tall chairs, I can see the whole room, totally packed. In all directions, a sea of people stretch out wall to wall.

The moment I've prepared for has arrived. I'm focused on my desire to autograph books for those who are lucky enough. I take my special calligraphy pen for signing out of my jacket pocket. It's my ceremony before the ceremony. Bring them on now!

Sitting here, I remember this morning just before I climbed into the van, Noi had explained, "There are three hundred tickets and only those people who can present their ticket will be able to have their books signed! You and Benz will only sign for two hours."

Three hundred in two hours! I never imagined I could manage to sign that many – or even have a reason to sign that many books in my whole life. Noi had also explained, "You'll be here to sign again, two days from now."

I think I'll have to keep my messages short. I decide to start out with, "All the best! Nelson." That seems a bit unfriendly but doing that three hundred times seems like a lot. I don't want a case of writer's cramp either. I'll try it short and expand on it if I have more time to do a longer one.

Oops! I'm on! A book just arrived.

I feel tense as I'm handed *The Real Alaska,* Benz's book with a chapter about me. I sign on the inside empty page and hand it to Benz. He's just finished signing *First Time In New York*. I sign on the same page as his and hand the book to the owner. I'm given another book, we sign and we trade again, but with this one, I'm also given a copy of *Giraffe* magazine. I check with the owner. He wants me to sign on the cover beside the huge picture with my necktie that looked like I was vomiting it up.

I notice in the middle of this, there are countless photos and videos being taken of the two of us doing the signing. We don't have to have a special pose for those and I lose awareness of it, even as background.

All that signing is an intense two hours for each of us, and by that time, I'm even signing books with no ticket. It was like becoming an efficient machine on an assembly line. We each manage to sign the three hundred copies of his two books. At the same time, I also signed nearly a hundred of the first issues of *Giraffe* magazines.

While signing, I receive gifts of drawings, and even a flower bracelet, Then it's Noi's voice: "time's up."

Benz and I are again surrounded by our escorts and we exit much the same way we entered – through the vast nearly silent crowd. A most unusual display of courteous admiration. I was so genuinely impressed with the orderly gathering and respect shown by a crowd that might have required police intervention in New York.

We all go back to the studio and later out to a restaurant for dinner together.

I'm tired. But I'm very happy too, for those who have their book signed - very happy indeed.

# 37

## *SWELTERING*

AT TEN IN THE MORNING, I'm picked up by the fully loaded van and taken out on the mostly four lane local roads. As we continue toward the outer limits of Bangkok, I notice large highways, perhaps six lanes, with carefully pruned hedges continuing for miles. Above this highway is a superhighway supported by beautifully designed single columns. It's very elegant design and as I'm told, a very efficient way to travel by car.

The next day at dinner with Vichai, he tells me, "Nelson, when I moved out to our house farther from the center of Bangkok, I drove the roads at ground level at first – mostly four lanes. They took two hours to get home. They were crowded, like the one yesterday. It was much faster, and it was worth it to pay the fee for the super road. It wasn't much money, and I made it home that way in one hour – a lot easier driving too."

Although I've given up driving, I hope Manhattan and Brooklyn get highways like that, especially ones that lead to the airports. I doubt if that will happen in my lifetime, however. Building new extensions on the subway lines is the current focus here in the Metropolitan area.

As the morning passes, we continue on smaller roads until we arrive in what appears to be a sparsely developed suburban area. Small older houses, many without glass in the windows sit back from the road. We turn onto a narrow, two-lane black top road, sparsely traveled by cars and motorcycles. Progress is steady for another twenty minutes until our van turns into a parking area with several small houses.

In front of these houses near the road, there are two trees with enormous trunks. One of them has a ribbon tied around it's trunk. I ask Benz, "why is there a ribbon on that tree?"

"That ribbon is a sign it's a 'wisdom tree'. It can't be cut down. It brings good luck to people who need to know their winning Lotto number. That's why we came here. You'll get to see how it can do that . . . maybe."

Now I'm curious. I climb out of the van into a wall of heat. The rest of the crew is unloading the cameras and setting up for the shoot. Noi suggests, "Nelson, maybe you should stay in the shade for now. Getting set up here will take awhile."

And she was right, so I stayed under the shade cast by the two large trees. At least it wasn't under the direct sun but I was perspiring. It was becoming hotter with no let-up, either.

At first, I watched the crew setting up, finding just the right position for the camera. It was being located right at the edge of the tarmac on the road and in the direct sunshine.

I didn't envy him for that but just beyond where I was standing. I noticed a small, abandoned, red car, rather badly damaged with its crumpled nose and open door. It's perpendicular to the road and the front bumper is almost even with the edge of the tarmac road.

Unlike the rural roads in the US, I never see 'shoulders' on the Thai roads, at least, not on the ones I had the occasion to travel.

Clearly the car in the yard had been dragged or most likely, backed off to clear the road. This damaged car was the only evidence of an accident I saw in my six weeks in, and around the city.

I never heard any kind of siren either in Bangkok itself, or the surroundings. This was the only damaged car. Since there are almost no traffic lights, a huge volume of traffic, and apparently almost no accidents, I asked Vichai what he believed accounted for this.

He replied. "the driving rule is, don't hit anything." I thought he was kidding. I couldn't believe there weren't other rules. Without speed limits, stop lights or signs, traffic police, lines down the center of roads, and turn signals even by the drivers, and shoulders on most roads. I have come to believe he was not kidding. From what I did see, the Thai system appears quite effective.

In America, even with all our speed limits, signs, lights, stripes on the roads, shoulders, and traffic police in the big cities, every year the fatalities resulting from driving accidents are equal to the casualty count in collisions alone equal to the Korean War. The injuries in car accidents including pedestrians, bicyclists, and motorcyclists far exceeds the death toll. No one seems overly concerned about this record, except the injured and their relatives. Apparently, it's the cost of driving just as the growing deaths and injuries are seen as the cost of hunting and self-protection.

The van pulls into the far end of the parking area closest to the house where the other large trees are providing shade. The day is bright with sun pushing the temperature well into the nineties and over that.

At first, the shoot is located in the shade of the largest tree near the road. That helps for a while, at least, until the sun moved as the afternoon dragged on.

The camera man at the edge of the road is continually in the direct rays of the sun all afternoon. I'm sweltering in my dress jacket and at least part of the time for that shoot, I stand in direct sunlight.

In this episode on acquiring lucky numbers, my role was to come forward and rub my thumb on the tree to get the number of the winning lottery ticket. That was it. No lines.

Since I had no lotto ticket and I was only following the script, the additional luck arrived soon. We were brought back to the city in time for a very delicious Thai dinner.

And I had none of the work an actor usually has. Noi made sure my soaking wet jacket was dry cleaned, ready, and in time for the next day on camera. Now that feels like only a super star or a king gets that kind of special care. Wonderful! I think I'm becoming very spoiled.

# 38

## *THE AGONY AND JOY OF ACTING*

THE NEXT SHOOT IS SCRIPTED for a Lotto episode with a Shaman who can foresee the numbers of the ticket, or can arrange luck so their client receives a winning ticket. Of course, magic and luck are the ingredients being paid for.

Considering the relatively short time I had in Bangkok, I've gotten to see quite a bit of the city and the surrounding areas. In this instance, we arrive at a large residential building located in another suburban sector of the city. There's a vacant room available for our shoot on the third floor. Although it's located in a widely different area of the city, the material structure itself contains construction materials similar to the other buildings I've been seeing. I'm guessing it's also fireproof, or at least, fire resistant.

The room for the shoot is medium sized. After looking at the few prescription bottles and other remaining possessions of the previous owner, I guess the room was once used by a single woman, perhaps rather ill, and/or elderly. She had left a variety of containers suggestive of health issues, and what remained of objects such as clothes racks, were worn and quite dilapidated.

By the time the room has become available for the shoot, walls need paint, and repairs for rather large holes. I was told, it had been used for storage after she left, and the tenant following her had also recently moved. The decrepit room was then available for our use as a film studio. Only the electricity is still working, but only for the lights. No air conditioning. No running water. Ugh!

The room is set up with meager props suggesting that those who make work as Shamanic magicians may be poorly paid. I meet the actor who is chosen to play the part of a shaman seer. In this case, the fellow is to produce enough luck for me to get the winning number at Lotto. I'm playing my usual part as the gullible old farang geezer who believes this particular shaman can do it for him.

For this shoot, I'm required to sit on the floor cross-legged once again, in a breezeless space. The temperature is in the nineties outdoors. Inside, with lights and no cross ventilation, it's even hotter. By the time of the shoot, the photo lights are all on, and adding to the temperature. I'm slowly wilting and as usual, soaking wet to begin the shoot. As I sit on the floor, my body is gradually stiffening. My acting partner keeps 'going up on his lines', repeatedly. He's probably in pain too, but he doesn't give up, and neither does our director.

It seems endless. To make matters worse, my right ankle, which was pressed on the floor yet again, was complaining. It was a very intense pain. Benz repeatedly reminds me to sit up straight, and as I struggle to stay vertical, my muscles and joints began to rebel. My ankle pain was nearly intolerable. Standing up to relieve it at that point was not an option.

Then, I remember. In my martial arts days, many years ago, I had mastered the ability to overcome pain, including the bow on stage standing in fire. I managed an altered state for the show which ran for ten years on tour. This is certainly no worse. I'm grateful that I only manage to hold my position for the next hour until we finally finish the final take. By then, the day is gone. It's nearly dark.

I slowly manage to stand again, but I have a new problem. There's no water. The bathroom is out of order and it's been more than three hours since I had used the men's room. Recognizing my anguish, one of the regular staff volunteered to drive me back to the studio. And, as usual, my jacket was sent out to the cleaners again.

Thanks to the rescue, my pants didn't have to go with it.

# 39

## *WOULD I DO OTHERWISE?*

ONE DAY, ABOUT THIS TIME, Benz comes to use the extra bed in my hotel room. It's for a second time.

Vichai brings him over, and the two of them converse in Thai on the couch. I go on with my writing. An hour or so later, Vichai leaves to go back to work.

Benz and I then talk briefly. At the end of our chat, he confesses to me, "I'm very tired"

He explains, "I need the extra bed in this room. I can't get enough sleep if I go out to my place in the suburbs, and then get back to *Salmon House* to work. I have to use the subway, and then a bus both ways. It's at least an hour each way. I need to be at Salmon House most of the time."

I understand and I feel sorry he hasn't made more use of the room. That's why I had been given a double room.

He talks about needing to do some writing and didn't explain what it was. I have only guessed it had to do with the publication: *Mini Moore, TALKS WITH Mr. NELSON*, which came out soon after I returned to New York. I had no idea Benz was keeping such detailed information on my conversations. He probably has near perfect memory, something I've come to envy.

As we're about to stop and get some sleep, Benz says, "One other thing – would you be able to stay two more weeks to finish up some of the Episodes?

I immediately think of my ankle wounds. Both legs are still in the compression bandages. My right ankle's still very painful. I don't know whether my right ankle's fully healed yet. It could mean delaying the treatment if I stay. I might even lose the foot.

Everything is flashing through my mind. I remember I still have materials the Wound Specialist sent with me, so I could do a further treatment if that would become necessary. Maybe the wounds <u>are</u> healing – or not? I have very little pain, unless I press an ankle to the floor when I sit cross legged on a shoot. But I can feel the scabs on my right ankle through the bandage. My left ankle seems okay. Totally healed? Should I delay my decision – tell Benz I need some time to think about it?

He's sitting on the couch. He's waiting for my answer. My performances at the nursing home is over. Doctor's orders! Even if my ankles heal enough due to a condition with the circulation in my legs – no way for that now.

I remember!

In phone time with Lillian, she tells me, "Whatever you need to do will be ok."

I miss her . . . I just can't turn down this invitation,

"Sure Benz! That works just fine for me. Two more weeks it is!"

# 40

## *THE LEARNING CURVE*

THE NEXT EVENING, I ARRIVE in the office space from a shoot.

A woman who's been working at a desk and is dressed in a sheet, is crawling around on the floor. Did she suddenly "lose her marbles?" What's she doing rolling around on the floor with a sheet on her anyway?

Then I remember what Vichai said to me, "anything is possible here."

Several of the staff are a standing audience. And most of the others remain seated, but are casually observing her. No problem.

I'm puzzled however. It appears to me, everyone regards a staff member crawling around on the floor in a sheet, as normal.

I've seen workers get tired and lie down on the floor back of their chair and take a nap. I've gotten used to that. However, I finally ask several audience members what's going on. They inform me, "Oh, she's the ghost in the video tomorrow evening, you know, when we do the shoot on site."

Oh yes, that reminds me, I do have some lines to review in the morning. Everything **is** normal!

The next day, as we wait by the parking area beside the studio, it's still daylight. By that time, I'm feeling fairly secure with my lines. The crew is loading cases of equipment, cameras, lighting, sheets, pillows, and a blanket for the bed, as well as makeup and costume for the actress. Clearly, this is an elaborate production.

When the loading fills most of the van, I climb into my usual seat behind the driver. The rest of the crew travels by cars, since most of the van is filled with props. The site's more than an hour drive out to a narrow residential street lined with multistory residential buildings behind walls of high white fences.

I learn our room will be in a building with low rents and large numbers of residents. I'm told the one room apartments can serve for elderly retirees, college students, new-comers to the work force, and newlyweds. It's vacant for the evening, prior to preparations for a new tenant.

By the time we arrive on site, it's dark. There are a few dim street lights. The van and several cars are already parked on the narrow street a short distance from the building where we will perform. The cars and van have their headlights on to help us see during the unloading. I join in the number of trips in the near dark required to bring all the equipment and suitcases into the room.

The room is considerably smaller than the room used for the video of the shaman who gave lotto numbers. Both rooms are less than half the size of the residential hotel room where I sleep. The suitcases, boxes, lighting equipment, and tripods, leave barely enough room to work for those of us who will be acting, as well as the crew that handles lighting, and the preparations required by scenery people. In short, it's way too crowded and has no place to sit down, except a small bed which is being used for makeup, and a small space to unload the suitcases and boxes.

The bathroom is closet size, barely enough room for one person and smaller than any I had seen so far – barely big enough to turn around in. At least, in this one, the water is turned on and the door can be closed.

Like my hotel room and all the residential buildings I was in, here in Bangkok, there's a small balcony opening to the outside for fresh air, and it contains the air-conditioning system. The venting for it, as is usual in Bangkok, is located on the ceiling in the room. As I've discovered in my hotel room, it's a very efficient system, since cool air tends to sink downward without putting the occupants of an apartment in the direct way of the draft. In my estimation, this is much more efficient than most air-conditioning units in America where they're located in the lower part of the windows closer to the floor.

Just my luck again, however. This evening, the-air conditioning is turned off until the next regular tenant occupies it. I'm living the life of an actor again this time, not a king.

The man who made it available assured me, "This space is typical for students, newly married people just starting out . . . people without good jobs – and sometimes, the elderly."

Since I didn't see anyone near my age in my entire six week visit to Bangkok. I can only guess the elderly live in another part of the city, or simply don't reach an age that is usual in America. I understand the King, now deceased, was nearing my age.

Since the apartment is located quite some distance from transportation, I assume a tenant has a car, motorcycle, bicycle, or walks several blocks out to the larger road and hails a motorcycle taxi. The motorcycle taxis cost very little, but it adds up if there's a trip to get food very often. An elderly person would need to be quite fit to stay here.

While the lights, cameras, and sound systems are being set up, Noi is slathering white makeup on the face and arms of the ghost. The ghost/actress requires a very extensive makeup procedure, plus her ghost costume.

The bed is unavailable to sit on, much as I would have preferred the chance to rest. Consequently, I'm standing the whole time the preparations are underway. it seems like it's hours, but my sense of time may result from my early arrival. I didn't wear a watch as part of my costume, so my only way to tell time during my stay in Bangkok was the wind up clock in my hotel room. I don't recall having a clock in my Samsung smartphone.

While all the considerable preparations are underway, I spend my time standing around waiting while the space was being turned into a studio.

When the set-up is well along, I'm given my lines again. I stand to the side of the room to re-read them. I used them to refresh my memory, having studied them well the day before. Also by this time, the camera setup is underway, sound is being wired on the ghost as well as on me, and the lighting setup is all tested and ready. Finally, the ghost sits on the edge of the bed for the remaining touch up. She is now totally white from head to foot.

Finally, the shoot is ready, the air-conditioner is turned off to prevent interference with the sound system during the shoot. The lights in the room are turned down low, and I'm directed to lie in bed with a sheet covering me. I'm already perspiring profusely in my costume. Unfortunately, the air-conditioner is off to prevent interference with the sound system. As I lay there, soaking under the sheet, the lights are turned almost off and the ghost appears in the doorway to the bathroom. There are a number of 'takes' and then the room light is turned on while the next set-up is being created. I'm still soaking in the bed.

For the next scene, the lights are dimmed again and I'm sitting up in bed while the ghost and I exchange more lines . . . and act more takes . . . and even more takes on each scene. However, I enjoy working with her. She's a very good partner, and I enjoy our time on camera. I never did find out if she went on with her acting, or this experience was quite enough for one lifetime.

When the session is finally finished, a considerable time is devoted to removing the Ghost's makeup and returning her to this life. Totally soaking wet, I stand and wait, and stand and wait some more while the equipment's packed up and taken back out to the van and cars for transport.

Finally, all except the sheets have been removed. Otherwise, the room is nearly empty except for some containers for photo equipment. Noi is last to leave and strongly suggests I lie down under the sheets in the bed and remain there while the entirety of the crew helps bring the equipment to the studio. When that is finished, I understand they get to go to their homes. As Noi prepares to leave, she tells me, "Leave the light on until I get back."

At the door, she tells me "I'll take care of some things. I'll be back to pick up the suitcases and bring you back to the hotel." She leaves the light on, and the door clicks shut.

I lie there under the sheet. I feel totally alone, abandoned. It's utterly silent. If anything happens, I have no information that allows me to know where my hotel is. What if they don't come for me tonight? I don't even know the hotel name or phone number. I have no idea where I am in the city of Bangkok. I only know a few people and all of them are away. I realize I haven't a clue how to call a motorcycle taxi or taxicab. I can't tell them where to take me, even if they understand English. I feel disoriented and totally helpless. It's like my childhood when I was tucked into bed and required to stay there until my parents came to get me up.

Suddenly, I realize, these feelings of being abandoned, alone, and helpless are based on my own early experiences. I now need the adult Nelson present to establish my adult feelings of responsibility and control. As this awareness crosses my mind, I remember I do have a Samsung cell phone. I can call one of the five members of the staff instantly if I choose. I can ask questions about my circumstances at the time I'm calling. Also, it suddenly becomes clear, I'm here for a reason, not because of my age and should rest up now after a long day. This is my job at the moment. It's because I'm needed here while the others are now free to meet the requirements of their respective jobs.

I also realize this room was rented for the shoot. It was vacated prior to preparations for the next tenant occupancy. As I lay in bed, I also remember I'm the current occupant. The remaining equipment was left in here along with me. By having me stay, the room has a light on and a person there. If anyone comes by and checks, it's occupied and therefore, not abandoned. I feel in control again and an important part of the crew after all.

Noi finally returns with several of the office staff to pick me up along with the remaining equipment and a suitcase, all of it destined to go back to the studio. By then, I've been of use. I'm the guard she trusted to leave behind. I was free simply to be there and relax.

When we leave the building, we go to a nearby restaurant for a very large and pleasurable Thai dinner. Many of the crew have arrived there and we enjoy a very good dinner. Afterwards, Benz is dropped off at the subway. Even though we are quite far out in the suburbs, he lives a considerable distance away and takes the subway to return home.

It's well after midnight when I'm taken back to my hotel room.

# 41

## *THE ACTING LESSON*

THE GHOST SHOOT ISN'T THE only time I had a heads up for an approaching shoot. Another occurs toward the end of my stay in Bangkok. I'm sitting on the couch and Vichai is in the leather covered overstuffed chair beside me. He tells me, "You have the opportunity to work briefly with Mr. Amporn."

"Who's this Mr. Acorn," I ask, thinking he had mispronounced the name.

And Vichai says, with a slight smile, "he's a famous actor here in Thailand."

I don't look impressed. I think he's probably just some poor actor they've found who will struggle with his lines while I sit on the floor again. Who am I to complain since I need a teleprompter to do my lines.

"Famous for what," I ask.

Vichai stares at me. "You know, like Mr. Bodin."

"I don't know who a person named Mr. Bodin might be, maybe, some poet – maybe a film maker? I don't know."

Vichai looks at me like I must be putting him on. That isn't helping me remember anything. Apparently I'm supposed to know the name of the famous actor I played a scene with two weeks before. Actually, as I think about it now, that would be something most actors would know.

I respond with, "so tell me."

Vichai, again with a slight smile, says, "he's the guy who's famous for playing the monk, you know, in the monastery scene about changing names."

"Oh, him, so yah, what about him?

"Well, Mr. Amporn is very famous for playing tough guy parts also. You'll see him tomorrow."

I feel like saying, "Thank you for warning me," but decided I'd play it cool and just sit tight. Maybe he's a great martial artist or something. Now that I've been reminded I've played opposite him, I do remember him. But a tough guy part too? It's hard to feel all that impressed. Maybe he's not just another actor. Vichai seems to believe he can play two very different kinds of characters. I hope he can meet Vichai's expectations. Tomorrow will tell.

The next day, as we turn into a narrow alley a quarter of a block from the studio, it looks deserted. No motorcycles, no cars, and no traffic. No people walking around either. The alley's lined with fences, some of them forming a head high wooden wall, having been painted white sometime, long ago.

It's late afternoon. We form a procession with Noi, Benz, Vichai, and the camera crew. The soundmen and I bring up the rear. We're scattered across the narrow alleyway, since there's no traffic. We're ambling along as if it's a holiday. It's a very long block.

I have the feeling it's a place I would have avoided if I were alone. By the time we've ambled midway down the alley, I'm noticing a short muscular man in worn blue jeans, lounging against a tall fence. If he had been in any alley in Brooklyn, I would have turned around and found a different route, even though I had taught Tae Kwan Do for a quarter of a century back when I was quite a bit younger. The most important thing I learned with all my training is, I can't move faster than a speeding bullet.

Even from a rather long distance, I can feel Mr. Amporn is a tough guy. That seems strange if he's played the monk only two weeks ago, as Vichai had said. Mr. Amporn is turning the action of casually passing time into a menacing act – more in the way a gangster would casually wait for the right victim to come his way, or more likely, make a deal to do a murder for hire.

Back in Brooklyn, I lived in a neighborhood where my two close neighbors had each killed a man on separate occasions, while I was living there. Both of them went to jail.

This was looking all too familiar. I was wanting to know for sure, this was not someone else who just happened to be in the alley where Mr. Amporn was supposed to be.

As we approach Mr. Amporn, he remains in his 'leaning posture' against the fence. He stands his ground and doesn't move. He glares as though we are intruders.

I begin to wonder if he actually works for a mob somewhere nearby and he's just humoring Vichai by playing an acting part on a moonlighting gig. I'm quite sure Vichai is putting me on about being the same person I worked with two weeks ago.

As I stand on his side of the fence, I have the strong feeling I'm really intruding on Mr. Amporn's turf. It's especially awkward because the crew with me is beginning to set up the cameras relative to the position Mr. Amporn seemingly has chosen. No one is talking to him or even looking at him. And no one has gone up to shake hands, including Vichai. They all remain on the other side of the street and don't even glance at him.

Meanwhile, I'm on his side of the alley and I continue to face him. If he's not an actor, he would come up to indicate we aren't welcome. A famous actor, if indeed it really is him, and I'm not even going up to him to introduce myself. If Mr. Tough Guy really is Mr. Amporn, it's hardly the way to greet him either.

After what was probably a short time, five minutes perhaps, Vichai must have realized my discomfort, or Mr. Amporn's. Vichai comes across the alley and brings me over to him to introduce me. "Mr. Amporn, your acting partner, Nelson Howe."

There's no change in Mr. Amporn's expression. I approach him and stop within arm's reach. He doesn't move and continues leaning on the fence just as he had since we arrived. He continues glaring at me with full eye contact. I don't move either and return the gaze. I wait for him to make the next move. He finally steps free of the fence with his hand extended. We shake hands. He has a strong grip. I also sense a feeling of humor about him as we shake hands. He's acting a part. He's holding a pose, not breaking character. He's about to be on camera.

I realize I'm in a part also. I'm in costume, as is he, but a very different one. I'm in a costume that is different than any I saw in Bangkok. I'm in character as an 'old farang geezer'. I'm meeting him as my partner and a fellow actor. I'm reassured. I can depend on him to be in character while we play the scene.

I was right. We did a short scene together followed by several additional stills taken of us posing. It was very clear, I'm in the scene in my own way too, just differently. He and I smile as we say goodbye. Acting is about holding character, no matter who we are, famous or not.

# 42

## *Very Sweet but . . .*

"SHE WORKS AS A SMILE," Vichai tells me before I meet her.

"A Smile," I ask. Vichai doesn't explain. I don't know what that means. I'm guessing in America she might work as a hostess in a nightclub or a salesgirl in a department store. I wait to meet her for the 'on camera' encounter and see what happens next.

We meet while the camera is being set up. She's very striking in her tight fitting all-red dress. We're being seated at right angles to each other, already in position for the video. We're both in character now in front of the camera.

The Smile is already going over her lines. She's quite tall, attractive, with an unusually small waist. I'm assuming it's a requirement for her work, whatever that is. The soundman wires each of us and somehow, to my amazement, he manages to slip the wire out of sight without interfering with her modesty.

In my case, it is the usual struggle to get the wire into my pants, up under my shirt and out to the knot in my tie. Wiring me turns out to be something of a performance for the crew, whenever and wherever it takes place. This is no exception.

I'm not sure whether the camera is running and all this is being documented or not, but her smiles are maintained for the entirety of the proceedings, hers and mine. I'm trying to do my best to look calm, cool, and collected. It's just in case my weird encounter with the sound man ends up as part of our feature on *You Tube*.

All the while, she and I make small talk until the lights are finally positioned, and the camera checked.

During this time, she tells me, "I'm the out-front representative for merchandise in sales settings." She assures me, "There are often other Smiles with their wares also. I present the prospective buyer with the benefits of the item being sold."

She explains, "My job requires standing all day smiling, whether I'm talking or not."

I'm impressed. It has to be a rather tough job. I didn't ask her how many hours a day she is required to stand there performing, but I'm guessing it's more than eight hours a day.

As we're chatting, I'm seeing an example of her at work, She's in character – smiling. She never breaks character. Never! I look away and glance back. I see she's smiling. The cameraman is asking for a slight change of her sitting position and she's smiling. The camera is having me shift slightly closer to her and she's still smiling. I find myself wondering if she smiles while she's asleep.

I smile a lot myself but I can look more serious too. Being in character on camera is easier for me since I can have more than one or two expressions. I'm quite sure I'm not smiling when I'm sleeping. I can't absolutely guarantee I never smile in my sleep, but my wife has never said I do. I decide not to ask Smile if she smiles in her sleep. It seems a bit too personal for the meeting we're having.

Just then, I hear,

"*Lights!*

*Ready!*

*Action!*"

She's saying her lines directly to me now, in Thai. I don't understand a single word. It seems to me it's a very long monologue. She talks very fast and never stops smiling. I guess it must be something about what she does for her living. I'm impressed because she remembers her lines very well. She must have to learn a lot of lines where she works. It's the way an actress works, but she's doing it for sales too. She continues to smile, sit straight, keep eye contact with me, and appears to be telling me something she wants me to know. It's an amazingly long monologue.

It's as if she's on camera all the time, whether the camera is on or not. I see her as a very professional actress, whatever her paid job is.

After several takes, it's my turn and I'm asking questions, as though I'm interviewing her. She continues smiling and laughs spontaneously, sometimes as if we were off camera.

Then we come to a part of the script where I say, "Can I grab your boobies?" I reach my hand in that direction.

She's been instructed to lose her smile at that moment while she slaps me hard across the side of my face.

I say my line but she freezes and can't slap me. I stop my gesture short of contact. It was in the script and part of her practice, but she seems very upset. She seems embarrassed and has lost her smile.

We attempt it several more times with the same result each time. She goes completely out of character. She's being instructed to hit harder and not to smile. She confesses she's afraid to hurt me. I realize she's spent her life seeing an old man, especially an old farang geezer, as someone who deserves major respect, almost like a monk. I am old, but I'm not a monk, even though I am an ordained Buddhist. She doesn't know that.

I tell her it's alright to slap me. One of the staff demonstrates what needs to happen. Apparently, she would tolerate being groped rather than slapping me to prevent it.

We rehearse again. She seems back in character.

"Action!"

We try it again on camera, she succeeds in a very feeble little love tap.

She's out of character and being the person who is living behind her façade as the 'Smile'.

I realize, I'm being spared the difficulty of actually carrying out my stated intention to grab her breast. She is able to stop smiling, but finds it too difficult to slap hard enough to be convincing, even though I reassure her I have been hit often much harder than she will, even when she tries.

I'm having two feelings. I'm liking her for feeling so reluctant to hurt me, but I'm feeling sorry for her too. She is so perfect in her acting, except for being able to give this old farang geezer a good hard slap in the face for acting so rude.

Later we're saying our good byes and she again apologizes for having hit me. I'm assuring her I'm unhurt and I understand her difficulty overcoming her natural kindness. As we leave, she is smiling – and, so am I.

# 43

## ANOTHER ADVENTURE

NOI COMES OVER TO MY couch. After her greeting, she asks, "Would you like a massage?"

I hesitate. "I'm not sure."

"It's free," she continues. He's very good.

"Okay, I'd like that, but there's still a possible problem – I have bandages on legs up to my knees. Do you think the massage could be a problem?"

"He's very good," she responds. "I'm sure he can work on you without a problem." Noi had made a similar positive statement when my front bridge fell out. The Thai dentist did it perfectly and it's still perfect as I write this.

"Okay, when?" I ask. I'm thinking I should go back to my hotel room and wash down. I don't have time to consider before she answers.

"Let's go," and Noi is holding her cell phone up speaking with someone as I'm following her out. I'm too embarrassed to tell her why I want to go back to my hotel room. What if I'm not going to wear my clothes for it? Or what if he has me wear clothes he has? I'm not sure I'm clean enough, but it's already too late. I take a chance.

Noi says it's a Thai massage. I have no idea what they're like. I once had my back walked on in one of the studios in Manhattan. I don't think it was Thai though. Who knows what could happen? Maybe I'd be pounded on. That happened once also. It might be similar to Swedish, which I had been trained in. It might also be more like the Chinese system to increase energy, the kind of pressure point massage I had that

111

done often in Chinatown when I was younger. I'm quite sure it isn't a Tantric massage which I'm adept at, but I keep it secret. I've got to stop guessing. Whatever it's going to be, I'll find out soon enough.

The van's waiting and a few minutes later we arrive at the place where I'm to be worked over, or on, rather. As we wait outside for a few minutes, Noi says, "he's usually . . ." I'm not sure what she said.

A few moments later, I'm in a little curtained off room on a massage table, flat on my back. In very clear English, He's asking me, "do you have any physical problem?"

I assure him, "only my legs," as I pull up my pant legs for him to see the compression bandages from my feet all the way up to my knees.

As I'm considering whether to discuss this further, he's getting some clothing from a little closet. "Put these on please."

He hands me a top and long pants. "Also, you can leave your underpants on, or you can use these if you want, or. . ."

As he re-enters the little curtained room again, I'm already out of my clothes, including underwear, and have gotten into the pants and shirt. I'm lying on the table on my back. As I'm wondering what he's going to do next, he's already putting pressure on the arch of my left foot with his cupped hands. He's not hurting me. I'm ok.

He begins with a strange alternating motion with one hand and the other. Sort of a griping pressure and as it lets go in one hand, it increases up beside it with the other. I picture it as a walking process up my legs but somehow, he avoids my ankle area. No pain, and no risk to my injuries. In fact, they've improved. He continues all the way up to my hip. I'm feeling an increase in energy in my left leg as he is beginning my right one.

I'm thinking it's a very effective method and it's pleasurable too. I'm relaxing and losing myself in the sensations of the massage.

I'm hearing, "turn over," and realize he's done my arms and front of my body already. I try to decide, either I'm partly asleep or I'm deeply in the sensations of the massage, or possibly both.

Next, I'm hearing, "take your time, now. Come out when you're ready."

I wasn't sure I would be ready anytime soon, but muscles are beginning to have their own life, and very shortly they move me to sitting up. I realize I'm actually enjoying my muscles moving me. Then I'm getting into my street clothes.

I thank my masseur, and he wishes me well. Then I'm out on the little sidewalk in front and one of the people from the studio is there.

Noi is gone and I'm being assured "the van will be here in a few minutes. And how was the massage?"

"Wonderful," I hear myself saying.

Already we're traveling in the van and next, I'm going up in the elevator to my room in the hotel. I'm remembering the last words I heard were, "you'll want to rest up before dinner."

I plunk down on the couch . . . and an hour or so later, nearly miss my dinner.

# 44

## *IT COULD BE PEANUTS*

THIS PARTICULAR AFTERNOON IN THE middle of the week, I'm sitting on the couch looking at back issues of a variety of magazines in other languages such as French, and even one in Chinese. I give up trying to read either one. Chinese was out of the question and my college French course was a near disaster. I've forgotten most of the vocabulary. I was too stubborn to learn from my mother who spoke it fluently. So I'm sitting, waiting for the next activity, whatever that might be. I'm day dreaming too, remembering yesterday, a brief conversation with Benz, seeing Vichai's wife and baby boy, Vichai holding the little fellow who looks like a wisdom being, clear, calm, observant; a beautiful child.

Vichai comes sauntering over to my 'office'. My daydream vanishes as he stops in front of the overstuffed chair beside me. Standing there, with his eye contact and a slight turn of his head, he casually motions me to come with him. I pull myself out of the comfort of the deep, soft cushions and follow down the hall into an elevator. No conversation.

As if entering an ocean in a submerged tank, we sink down to another floor. The elevator door opens into a hall. We enter a nearly empty conference room with a large table surrounded by a number of chairs. I recognize the room. I've been here before when it was in use for a discussion with Vichai, and Noi.

After a short silent interval, Noi enters with a fresh coffee for me. I settle into a cushioned swivel chair while Vichai chooses a seat several chairs away. On this occasion Noi and I are seated beside each other.

She's munching on some little tan, beanlike objects, as she talks in Thai with Vichai.

After twenty minutes or so, without speaking to me, she leaves the room. I notice the paper sack with the beanlike objects is abandoned, right next to me. I continue to sip on my coffee which is cooling as the surface gradually sinks lower in my cup.

Besides my love of coffee, I have something of an appetite . . . and a growing curiosity. The bag is lying on its side. Its mouth is completely open. I can clearly see inside, and it's just close enough, as if inviting me to check the contents. Vichai continues working with the desk top video, makes brief small talk. Then he leaves also.

I'm sitting alone. I've reached the last remains of my coffee – and there sits the bag – mouth wide open. The little brown objects look quite edible, like chocolate. I think they would go perfectly with my remaining few sips of tepid coffee.

What to do? Noi is such a lovely person. I decide she probably won't mind if I sample a morsel of chocolate bean, or nut, or whatever it might be. I slip my hand into the open sack and trap something very small between my first finger and thumb. I put whatever it is in my mouth. I leave it sitting on my tongue as I begin to taste it. It has a slight salty taste, so I decide it probably is some kind of a nut common to Thailand. I bite down on it. It has a slight crunch on the outside as if it has a thin crispy skin but it also seems soft. As I chew it, I realize in has a flavor that I can't recognize. It's certainly not chocolate. And it's probably not a member of the nut family – too soft – and a completely new flavor. It definitely is not like anything I ever tasted. I hesitate to try another since Noi didn't suggest I help myself. Problem. Do I, or don't I? What should I do? After all, she is the Producer and in charge of the whole operation.

I take a sip of the remaining coffee while I try to convince myself that she won't mind if I take another. There's a slightly bitter after taste from the coffee and the little faintly salty nutlike object would be especially good after that. It has an intriguing flavor I can't resist.

I tell myself, she'll understand and my hand goes in and takes another little bean. I examine it carefully before I put it in my mouth. It feels slightly soft, but has a dry outside, like a skin. It's rather good, so

I try another. That leads to several more. By then the coffee is gone and I don't want Noi to be upset with me for eating too much of her treat.

So, I'm thinking now of what I'm going to say to her, but just then, she returns. I blurt out, "I only ate a few of the little beans – they are right here beside me and I couldn't resist. I'm so sorry. They tasted very good with the coffee. But I can't recognize what they are. I've never eaten anything quite like that before."

Noi just looks at me with no expression and doesn't answer.

I feel very guilty for not asking permission to taste them. I'm afraid I said too much, or maybe she is angry with me for tasting her food while she was out of the room, especially when I didn't ask permission.

Noi remains standing and seems to be thinking of something else, perhaps something she wanted to say to Vichai. I'm almost relieved. Then she looks directly at me. As she picks up the sack and turns to leave, she replies matter-of-factly, "silkworm larvae."

I'm relieved. But shocked too. I ate larvae? They don't have silkworm larvae in America. In America it's unimaginable to eat them – but they're really quite good! I think I'll stick with milk chocolate for now, however.

# 45

## *VICHAI PROVES HE'S PSYCHIC*

I HEAR NO MORE ABOUT the noise problem in the restaurant scene with the waitress until the middle of my last week in Bangkok. As often happens, I'm lounging on the couch to be available for the next project.

Vichai saunters up to my imaginary 'office' and casually motions me to come with him. It's almost as if he expects me to have other plans.

I get to my feet and follow him through several halls to an office space with a video monitor and keyboard set up.

He has me sit down in a swivel office chair beside him. He plays a short segment of a video containing several pieces of very contemporary music. He asks, "you like the music?"

"I think I liked the second one better. Maybe play it again?" So we listen again.

Vichai looks at me as if he has a question.

Without hesitation, I answer, "Second one, for sure. I like it. It's unusual."

He nods agreement. We discuss it briefly and he explains, "It's background, maybe for one of the programs, maybe even for the six episodes we've been doing."

I'm wondering what he's up to now, but I don't ask.

Vichai takes out the microphone we used on camera, reaches over and he pins the microphone on the outside of my tie.

Now he's got my attention! It's never been pinned on the **outside** of my tie, ever!

We've gotten to know each other and I know he'll explain what's happening, and sure enough, he starts.

"That scene in the restaurant was too noisy to hear you," he explains. "We have to do the sound over again".

"I see," I say casually. I remember the noise in the restaurant and having to abandon the shoot.

He pauses and then says, "Fine then. Say your order to the waitress the way you did in the restaurant. I'll play your order for you now. You can just say the lines in your head this first time. Then I'll play it again and you speak them just the way you see your mouth moving in on the screen. Ok?"

I nod a 'yes.'

He plays the scene again for me.

"Well," I admit. "I have a problem."

"What's that," he asks, as if he has no idea what that problem could be.

I confess, "I don't seem to remember the lines, even when I'm seeing me saying them on the monitor."

He smiles. "Make a guess."

I can't believe he can be so relaxed about this. I decide it's worth a wild guess in case <u>he</u> doesn't know the words. "It went something like this," I say. "I want a slice of pizza, no pepperoni and no anchovies. I want the something or other on the side" I sit silent for a moment, "and I don't remember the rest."

"Well, let's have a look," he says, as he starts the scene.

He plays it several times and then recites the lines just by watching me do it in the video. I'm amazed. Even though there's no sound of my voice, he says the whole line I had used to order the food. I realize why he seemed psychic in the hotel that day. I'm very impressed. He repeats the sentences several times until I can say the lines fast enough to try it with the picture.

I finally can repeat the words, but some of the words were emphasized more than others.

Vichai says, "now all you have to do is to say it exactly the same speed, exactly as you are saying it on the video – only louder."

I try it.

Then he says, "faster."

I speed up.

He says, "it sounds memorized. Now do it like you're there talking to the waitress."

And so it went, until he finally agrees, "it's close enough."

"But doesn't it have to be even closer to the way I said it there," I ask.

Vichai smiles. "Yes, you're right. We can get a guy who can shorten or lengthen the sound a fraction of a second, so it will sound just the way it looks. Don't worry."

If he says so, I certainly won't lose any sleep over it – and I haven't yet.

# 46

## MY VISION OF A MASS KIDNAPPING

DURING THIS LAST WEEK, I'VE been gradually preparing myself to leave. I'm already starting to feel the sense of loss. It's the nagging sense that something very special in my life is being left behind.

If I didn't have Lillian and a number of close friends in America, I might be tempted to work out a way to stay in Bangkok. But I don't speak enough Thai to manage without the very special care I've become accustomed to having during my visit. That kind of care is truly a very precious gift.

I also know I have to say my goodbyes now. Each person I have worked with is precious, a friend who I may not see again in this lifetime. That's especially hard to think about. Every time I put another shirt in my suitcase, I feel the deep sense of loss. Whenever I'm in the studios or even go to lunch across the street, I know it's another goodbye. It's only a matter of a few days before our final goodbyes.

For me, it's all become very touching. The office work groups have given me gifts and we've all had our group pictures taken. It's very sweet of them. I've become fond of the whole crew and wish I could have them all back to New York City with me.

Most of my belongings are already packed now, the gifts from the staff, original drawings for the books they've created and designed, original work from the Book Fair, and photos. It feels so hard to leave such love behind. I'm sad now each morning as I stand looking out over the city I've come to love – knowing it's possible I will never see it again.

I'm sitting in my make believe office on the couch ruminating on the joy of my visit. Suddenly, Noi comes in. I get up from my place on the couch and greet her with my usual "hi" which she returns with a fond smile. So now's my chance to take her to dinner, at last.

"Is there a particular place where you're fond of dining, Noi? My treat."

She smiles and replies, "Oh, that will be nice!" She's already taking her cell phone out.

It happens superfast, and as we arrive at the street, I ask again, "any place in particular you prefer dinner?"

Without hesitation, she says, "let's go to the hotel dining room. It's close by."

I'm puzzled now, but I decide, who am I to second-guess her? As I'm thinking that, a car pulls up and stops in front of us.

"It's ours," she says.

It's late evening as we enter the empty hotel dining room. When we're seated, I look at the menu. I've only eaten one of the choices.

I confess to Noi, "I usually have this one when we're out, not out on a shoot. I'm willing to have some variety, since you know the food much better than I do."

Noi smiles, points to a picture on the menu, and asks, "would you be okay if we order this also?"

I agree. I trust her decisions.

Before she's done, I agree to three more courses, plus the appetizers, and a cup of coffee to wash it all down. By the end of our evening, I'm happily stuffed.

Along with the food, and the care, I treasure our chance for conversation. And needless to say, I don't touch any food with my fingers. But as I think back on our meal together, I don't think I was enough connected with my feelings to convey all the gratitude I actually have for all she had done for me. It would only be later, when I've returned to life in Brooklyn, I'm remembering all the ways she so generously looked after my safety and comfort.

The conversation ends with our understanding we want to stay in touch with each other when I return back to New York City. I was quite disorganized when I got back and there was at least a month or more when I neglected writing. In fact, it was shortly before Christmas before I managed to write.

# 47

## *How Did They Do It?*

THE DAY BEFORE MY LAST morning at breakfast, I finally solve a mystery.

During the week Lillian was here, we ate breakfast in the dining room. It was busy, very alive by eight in the morning. Also, during that time, there was a long buffet table against the far wall. It had all kinds of wonderful additions to our order to make a breakfast into a feast – fresh fruit including ripe watermelon and pineapple slices, a toaster for the tender fresh croissants, rolls and bread, fresh pour-your-own hot coffee, steaming hot chocolate, newly made strawberry jam and grape jelly, fresh milk, sugar, cream, and sweet fresh juices from the fruit grown in Thailand. My mouth waters just writing this.

And each morning at eight o'clock, we went over to that table and loaded up on the scrumptious offerings, as did everyone else who arrived to treasure the gifts.

That marvelous table was still there on Thursday morning, the day Lillian left for the USA. Friday morning, it was gone! Unlike the previous week, there's no one in the room for breakfast. I have the whole dining room to myself. I choose a booth with a partition near the back of the room so I'm not seen directly from the street, except from the side where the table had been. No one came by to look in anyway.

Because the buffet table filled with goodies was missing – gone. I was very disappointed. I began thinking of all the delicious gifts I would miss.

I began visualizing the table and remembering the taste of the butter covered croissants slathered with fresh strawberry jam. As I was salivating and in mourning for my loss, the waitress comes to take my order.

I decide she won't be able to fix it anyway and I'm resigned to the situation. I order my usual egg omelet with a salad and hot coffee. When my order arrived, my breakfast included all the wonderful extras. It had exactly what I had chosen from the table during the week while Lillian was there – the three fruits, three croissants, strawberry jam, a glass of fruit juice, and fresh coffee. Apparently, the staff had recorded exactly what I chose from the table each day we ate there.

On this, my next to last day at breakfast, the buffet table on the side of the room is back in place and the room is filling up with people as it had when Lillian and I were there together. Wonderful! This time, I don't need to go and make selections from the buffet table because I'm served exactly the same wonderful breakfast as I had without it. It even arrived on the last morning before I said my goodbyes.

During my stay, I was always treated as royalty. Just for example, in the hotel where I continued after Lillian left, no one who entered could have entry to the elevators until they were ok with the desk. The dining room was kept nearly empty the rest of my visit. My trips outside the hotel were always accompanied by at least one and usually two staff people from Salmon House to escort me. Even my room was changed soon after Lillian left. I was moved across the hall in a room with two beds. It would allow for Benz to have a place to sleep when he was working too late to get out to his room and get any sleep.

It's unbelievable I've become so spoiled – it's become very hard to leave.

# 48

## *MY LAST ADVENTURE . . . PERHAPS*

SHORTLY BEFORE MY FINAL DAY in Bangkok, Noi tells me Salmon House Bookstore suggests I do a book signing.

My self-interest is still in full gear, and I agree. The flight to Brooklyn will be long and lonely hours of drawn shades and only the light at my seat. I decide a book is an absolute necessity, and Salmon House Bookstore will be the perfect place to find it.

The next morning arrives and I'm scheduled for the pickup in an hour or two after my lunch so I have the morning off. I finish most of my packing before I'm taken to the bookstore with Benz and Vichai. The three of us are dropped off at the door. Benz goes off by himself and Vichai settles in to talk with someone he knows. I wander off into book-land for my intended treasure.

However, I feel more and more alone in a desert of books as I begin my wanderings. This is the biggest bookstore I've ever seen! While it's true, New York City has several multi-floor bookstores, none of them seem to stretch for blocks in all directions. It's gigantic, and in spite of walking toward what I thought would be the back wall, I never reach it. It turned out to be larger than I had imagined!

It's also lonely, almost deserted. Where are all the book buyers? There doesn't seem to be anyone I can approach with my questions.

As I began my wanderings further and further into the vast wilderness of books, I feel a strong need for a compass also. My gift replacement Samsung doesn't seem to have one. I'm lost on *Salmon House Book Planet,* and the books are all in the language of the world

I'm wandering around in. It's like a dream ocean made of books. Worse yet, this ocean is filled with books I can't read, and no one anywhere to ask if there are any printed in English.

Only the tops of heads appear in the distance. They disappear just as I finally find the isle they were in. I can't decipher the signs, all written in Thai. I can only guess they give directions to the various sections of the store where the particular books I might find interesting are printed in English.

As I continue my now directionless walking, I go into shock. It occurs to me . . . maybe, **there aren't any books in English!** And maybe, there aren't any shoppers.

I regret that I hadn't asked Noi for any suggestions about my intended book search. Or what should I be doing besides just standing still in utter confusion, trying to figure out, **what I'm doing here?**

In my increasing stupor, I wander farther and farther into the depths of the store. I'm assuming I would come ashore somewhere if I continue to wander long enough. There must be a cliff or a beach somewhere in all this vastness. I have no idea what time I'm to meet with the others, or even whether Noi will turn up to direct the occasion. All the shelves look alike now. Unlike Hansel and Gretel, I didn't have any breadcrumbs to leave as a clue to finding my way back.

I turn a corner in a desperate attempt to find at least one human close enough, and slow enough, to finally catch them. Suddenly, a cluster of four young Thai women approach me. Hooray! They're here in the same isle with me. At first, they act like they know me.

As I hurriedly approach them however, they seem unsure about that. I must appear as an 'alien being' from another planet. I'm still wearing my costume. I'm not sure about them either. As we stand looking at each other, I try to understand them, but they're speaking Thai.

I ask, "do you speak English?" Several leave to go look at more books.

The one who seems to think I look familiar tries to speak to me in Thai. I tell her in English, "I don't speak Thai." She shakes her head and looks more puzzled.

I'm trying to think of a way to help her, so I ask, "Have you seen *BKK 1ˢᵗ Time* on *You Tube*?"

With that, she now seems even more puzzled. We both give up, and she walks in the direction of her three friends, shaking her head like she's just met a creature from Mars. I continue wandering aimlessly, feeling as if I'm the one who just met the Martian who didn't want to be found out.

I'm feeling totally lost. Still no books in English, no wall to follow, no Benz, no Vichai, no Toast, and no Noi.

**Help!** I want my space ship! Better yet, I want all of them to come and rescue me.

Suddenly, my cellphone comes to mind. I could call one of them and say I'm lost. Of course when they find out I'm in the same store where they left me, they will have a problem finding me. They can't find me here any more easily than I can find them.

Another hour goes by as measured in earth time. I finally see a young man and as I make eye contact, he stops in his tracks, then approaches me acting very excited and asks, "you, John, John, John?"

I nod a 'yes,' as I've learned to do here.

He tells me, "I play *BKK 1ˢᵗ Time* on my cellphone every day!"

I'm impressed. He also speaks very good English.

He's holding his cellphone and asks, "can I take your picture with me?"

I think, wonderful, Nelson! Look at the good side! Human life here again – a real admirer! He can even get me out of here.

"Sure," I answer confidently.

He sidles up and extends his hand with the camera out in front of us as he tries to get both faces in the frame. He cuddles up closer, almost touching my face with his and pulling me in tight with his free arm. He seems very strong, and determined. Now he has both of us in the picture. I'm thinking I like being photographed better with young women, and where are Vichai, Benz, and Noi anyway? Even Book and Bank aren't here.

My admirer now decides he wants me to pose with the curse word I used at the end of the video. I'm in the mood big time now. He has no idea! I readily agree, so he pulls me in tight again and we both pout like we're about to kiss someone and . . . **click**. He brings his arm close and informs me that he wants both our faces to show more so he pulls me in closer yet and we pout again, as I'm thinking of the swear word I would like to say out loud, and this time, he gets the shot.

As he lets go, I ask him, where's the front entrance from here? He points in the opposite direction from the way I've been going and rushes away before I can find out if I just go straight in that direction or have to turn off somewhere.

Too late. I'm sure I made some other turns to get here. I stand still considering the situation and wondering if this is just the price of fame, or I'm having a bad day . . . or both, apparently!

As I wander for what seems like several more days, two young women approach me. They're very excited and recognized me instantly. At last, I'm back on this planet and the two take turns, snuggling me and operating the camera. They thank me in English for letting them enjoy my stardom and both turn to leave.

I return a "have a good time" and immediately ask which direction to the front of the store. They must be twins, or at least sisters who are close in age since they seem to be hitched together and point in unison towards the direction I was going.

I'm so relieved to be heading toward shore . . . I mean someplace where people know me and speak English again.

I finally stagger past another row of books and find myself at the cashier's table. I had never had such warm, fuzzy feelings for a cashier table before in my life. Better yet, several people there even seemed to know me.

Regrettably, I couldn't remember where I might have seen them before, let alone remember their names. It turns out it doesn't matter. They welcome me and assure me Vichai will be here soon and so will Noi, and even Benz. They bring a large table and several chairs where I'm to sit while I sign books . . . and more books.

Noi arrives with several staff members and soon after the signing is underway, Vichai comes with a pile of books entitled *Real Alaska* written by Benz Thanachart Siripatrachai to sign for *Salmon House Publishing*.

And when I'm finally beginning to meet my fans, they're having me sign their book and have their selfies with me. In short, I stay very busy. After an hour or more, the crowd thins out, but by that time, I had more piles of books that needed signing. I was told there was a popular band playing just down the stairs from the bookstore so people were going there. At least I get to sit down.

The band finally gets exhausted, and a now devoted crowd of more than sixty suspects gathers all across the front of the book store. A steady stream of people come in for a book to be signed and selfy-fied, so it's become a 'sign a book and cuddle time.'

Finally, Noi says, "Time to stop." The crowd suddenly doesn't seem to understand Thai any more. Signing and cuddling goes on non-stop in that order. I manage to bend over to sign. Between pouting to do the swear word with the appropriate symbolic finger language with each selfie, and smiling for the selfie, I barely can speak. I began to want to sit down again.

Finally, Noi suggests I come out in front of the table and do the Thai dance. It's the one that had seven hundred thousand followers when it was first on *You Tube*. Because of my bandages and Doctor's orders, it had been nearly six months since I had practiced it. It seemed to me, it was more like a decade since I had performed it.

Noi turns on the video to *You Tube* so I could hear the music for the dance. The monitor was in back of me so I still couldn't see what I had done half a year ago. None of it came to mind. I'm unable to remember a single move. I improvise a totally new dance with a few remembered moves toward the end. It was apparently a show-stopper, quite literally.

To faint applause, everyone leaves, including all of us.

I never thought about finding a book again until I took my seat in the plane, several days later.

# 49

## *EVERYTHING?*

I END UP ON MY couch one more time. It's goodbye to my pretend office. At least I think so. No more time on camera, but why am I sitting here instead of going back to the hotel? It's been a long last day. Everything is ready for the editing. Everyone must be waiting for the magical appearance of a backer.

I sit here waiting for my ride back to the hotel. The studio's silent, empty of the regular staff tonight. They've finished their projects and gone off to grab some sleep for their next day's work or more likely, take a day off. I hope someone might remember I need a ride back to the hotel.

Of course, I needn't worry. I remember, no one has forgotten to get me back to the hotel for the entire six weeks. My mind wanders and I remember I haven't seen Benz since afternoon either. I wonder where he went – maybe home to get some much-needed sleep.

I'm wondering why I don't seem to have acquired magic after all my adventures here in a country that has so much of it.

As I think about it, it occurs to me, maybe I've had magic my whole visit here. Workers brought breakfast when we got dressed. Benz added me to his film which won awards. He starred me in a TV video that drew millions to it. I was given six weeks in Bangkok and made at least seven or eight videos. I thought it was a magical world here. And here I am feeling sorry for myself.

Grow up, John, John, John, Nelson!

I assure myself, if I really have the magic, I could be in two places at once. I wouldn't have a twenty-four-hour air flight to deal with. I could win a lottery or two. I could become a man of leisure. I might even speak Thai!

But now that I've come to think of it, I've become famous overnight. I'm loved by hundreds of thousands of people, just because I'm here. Just for being me. It's what my mother wished for me. Here it is!

And here I sit, living my fantasy life. And this is part of it too. I've said my final goodbyes to the staff who've left me with their drawings, books, and hugs for the evening – all except Noi, and Vichai. I think Noi has left already, and Vichai will come to take me back to the hotel, at least I hope so. As I sit here, I'm thinking about my flight tomorrow.

I hear footsteps, at last.

"Hi Noi! What's that?" She's carrying a large white cover book cradled in front of her with both arms. It's at least two inches thick and nearly a foot tall.

I stand up and greet her. I'm about to ask her, "What kind of a book do you have there?"

But before I can ask her, she hands it to me. "Have a look," she suggests.

I flip it open. There's a full-page photo of me! I turn the page – there I am, in the studio, and here's a news program – and four pages of me at the National Book Fair!

"Wow! I can't believe this!"

Noi is looking very pleased. "I thought you'd like this as a going back to Brooklyn gift."

I'm nearly in tears. "It's wonderful!"

I feel so touched. I look at the front pages and all the newspaper and TV coverage is there, page by page. As I continue through the book, there are the on-site photos of me in the ghost shoot, the graffiti, and the tree I was rubbing for the winning lotto number. There are full page photos of the vast crowds of fans who met me at the National Book Fair.

"How did you get all that?" I'm amazed that everything I did for the six weeks, even signing books with Benz in the *Book Fair*, and dancing in the *Salmon Publishing Book Shop* that evening was photographed!

"I photographed everything you were doing,"

"You photographed me somehow, even in the thousands packed in at the National Thai Book Fair? I didn't see you doing that either."

"I was there while you were signing, and I did aerial shots from an upstairs window in the studio while you were doing your lines too."

I turn to her with tears in my eyes and bow as I do my wei. "This book is a treasure . . . and you are truly the gift I will never forget."

# 50

## *I WANT YOU ALL BACK AGAIN*

MY DEPARTURE DAY HAS ARRIVED. I'm riding one more time with Vichai. It's miles out of Bangkok to the airport. Toast is in the front seat with Vichai once again.

I'm seeing the City slipping past in the afternoon sun, as if it's energy is weakening. I know that feeling. It's my feeling, especially today as the sun too, slowly slips from its place in the sky.

And I'm remembering that time when day-after-day, people see me on the street, or in a restaurant, or a store, and come and hug me in welcome. It is as if the people of the great city of Bangkok are my brothers and sisters – and my children – we are part of each other's family.

The buildings grow smaller, and farther apart in the fading daylight. I feel the growing desire to have Vichai turn the van around and take me back. I want to be in two homes at once, here and yet I'm looking forward to being with Lillian again too. She's patiently waited for me to return to her, and I miss our times together.

As we drive, I'm silent. It's the end of a most wonderful adventure ever in my life. And I also know my life can never be like this again.

As the landscape slips by and the day begins to darken, I know I've been loved by millions of people, sometimes only for few moments, sometimes for a few days, and for a few, who have made this so extraordinary for months . . . and now, perhaps, forever.

As the landscape is finally open country, Vichai pulls our van into the parking area. I know there is no turning back. For that moment, time feels like the river that flows only in one direction. But I also know better. It's the limited product of my mind. I know I'm in being-time that has no boundaries, the dimensionless space where love can have no limits either.

# 51

# *THE GATE IS THAT WAY*

WE'VE ARRIVED. AND FOR ONE more time, there's wonderful Noi again with a whole host of the staff. I feel I want to embrace everyone. I want to bring them all back to New York City. I feel so possessive of everyone in Thailand.

I even want to apologize to that lonely bird, the poor winged creature that kept calling to me as though asking for a hug, and a picture with me too. I'll miss the sound of all those darting creatures performing their supersonic aerial acrobatics for my entertainment after breakfast. But most of all, I want all my wonderful experiences, and everyone to come back with me.

I'm sure they will, as magical memories.

The whole gang of us, including Noi and Vichai, walk through the terminal toward the check-in and ticket center. I suddenly have no words, only the warm loving feeling of walking together with everyone.

And as we near the other side of the terminal, Noi and I find ourselves together and slightly behind the group. I'm thinking of the book of photos she had given me. I slow to a stop and turn to her, "thank you so much for all you've done for me. And now you've added the wonderful photo book. I can't believe you put that together and are giving me this gift too. It's a precious gift I will treasure for all the rest of my life."

We all hug and say our good byes, and as I finish, I hear Vichai call, "**Nelson!**"

He points to the window where I'm to check my suitcase and get my boarding ticket. As my suitcase is put on the conveyer belt, the woman who is handing me my ticket recognizes me and asks, "Can have a photo with you?"

"Of course," I reply. She's about to get up and come out in front of her station, but stops. Then she looks sad, hesitates, and reluctantly asks, "can you do that later? I can't leave my station."

I didn't know her and I will never see her again, but I will never forget her either. I feel sad she didn't get her wish.

We all move to the far side of the terminal where I and the group say our good byes and hugs of farewell. Vichai and I hug, wishing each other good luck one more time, and pointing, he says, "the gate's over that way," and he was gone.

# 52

## *HOME WITH LILLIAN*

HERE, I HAVE MY LILLIAN, my friends, and my adventures, dancing, and writing.

And I carry with me, all my wonderful memories of the wonderful Ms Nok and her daughters, sons, and grandchildren, and the National Book Fair . . . and a ride on a Taxi motorcycle.

And when someone who's seen my video calls out, **"John, John, John?" They mean Me – Nelson.** They always ask, "can I have a selfie with you?" And I always say "<u>YES</u>!"

And none of this could have happened without my Benz, and Noi and Vichai, Ms Nok, Salmon House and all my wonderful friends in Bangkok, and now, here in America too.

I miss all of you, the continual sense of being loved – and the joyous family of those who have made my visit such a super experience. And I miss the thousands who came to see me at the National Book Fair, the throngs of people who rushed to hug me, and especially the friends who I worked with. I wish you all a wonderful life and thank you for your most wonderful gift of a lifetime . . . all of you who made my adventures so glorious.

Here, in my castle of dreams, I relive the time in that fabled place with the fabulous people I know.

And now, I'm happily settled back in the magic of 'home again' in Brooklyn too, with my lovely Lillian, and my many good friends here – fondly dreaming of the past as we sit perched at the edge of the ocean – sending all our love from us – to all of you!

\*\*\*

Printed in the United States
By Bookmasters